Italy Today:
Patterns of Life and Politics

Edited by
Luisa Quartermaine
with
John Pollard

UNIVERSITY OF EXETER

First published 1985 by the University of Exeter
Second edition, 1987

© 1987 University of Exeter and the several
authors, each in respect of
the paper contributed

ISBN 0 85989 266 2

Printed in Great Britain by A. Wheaton
and Co. Ltd., Exeter

CONTENTS

ACKNOWLEDGEMENTS

We wish to thank our contributors, and also particularly Stephen Mennell for reading the articles and making several useful suggestions. We are also grateful to Barbara Mennell for assisting in editing and to Professor John Flower for his helpful comments and advice. We would like to acknowledge the generous support of the Italian Institute in London, through its Director Professor Alessandro Vaciago, and of the Western European Studies Centre of Exeter University. Their financial contribution towards the publication of the book was greatly appreciated.

The front cover of *The Overpass, Siena*, 1984, by Jeffrey Smart, oil and acrylic on canvas, 100cm x 70cm is reproduced by kind permission of Soma Gallery Lugano.

Luisa Quartermaine
Exeter, January 1985   John Pollard

ABBREVIATIONS

AC	Azione Cattolica
ACEC	Azione Cattolica Esercenti Cinema
ACI	Automobil Club Italiano
ACLI	Associazioni Cristiane di Lavoratori Italiani
AGI	Associazione Goliardica Italiana
CEE=EEC	Comunità Economica Europea= European Economic Community
CEI	Conferenza Episcopale Italiana
CGIL	Confederazione Generale Italiana del Lavoro
CIPE	Comitato Interministeriale per la Programmazione Economica
CIPI	Comitato Interministeriale Politica Industriale
CL	Comunione e Liberazione
Cs	Cosenza
CISL	Confederazione Italiana Sindacati Lavoratori
Cz	Catanzaro
DC	Democrazia Cristiana
EIAR	Ente Italiano Audizioni Radiofoniche
ENI	Ente Nazionale Idrocarburi
ESAC	Ente per lo Sviluppo Agricolo della Calabria
FDP	Fronte Democratico Popolare
FIM	Federazione Italiana Metalmeccanici
FINSIDER	Società Finanziaria Siderurgica
FIOM	Federazione Italiana Operai Metallurgici
FLM	Federazione Lavoratori Metalmeccanici
FUAN	Fronte Universitario di Azione Nazionale
GDIP	Giurisprudenza (Comparata) di Diritto Internazionale Privato
IACP	Istituto Autonomo Case Popolari
INAM	Istituto Nazionale Assicurazione Malattie
IRI	Istituto per la Ricostruzione Industriale
ISTAT	Istituto Centrale di Statistica
ITALSIDER	Società Italiana Siderurgia
MSI	Movimento Sociale Italiano
OCED=OCSE	Organizzazione per la Cooperazione e lo Sviluppo Economico
ONMI	Opera Nazionale Maternità e Infanzia
PDIUM	Partito Democratico Italiano di Unità Monarchica
PDUP	Partito Democratico di Unità Proletaria
PLI	Partito Liberale Italiano
PMP	Partito Monarchico Popolare
PNM	Partito Nazionale Monarchico

PPI	Partito Popolare Italiano
PR	Partito Radicale
PRI	Partito Repubblicano Italiano
PSDI	Partito Socialista Democratico Italiano
PSI	Partito Socialista Italiano
PSIUP	Partito Socialista Italiano di Unità Proletaria
PSU	Partito Socialista Unitario
RAI	Radio Audizioni Italiane
Rc	Reggio Calabria
UGI	Unione Goliardica Italiana
UIL	Unione Italiana dei Lavoratori
UILM	Unione Italiana dei Lavoratori Metalmeccanici
UNURI	Unione Nazionale Universitaria Rappresentativa Italiana
URI	Unione Radiofonica Italiana
USL	Unità di Sanità Locale

INTRODUCTION

Since the Second World War Italy has changed more rapidly and more dramatically than probably any other Western European nation. In less than forty years, it has been transformed from an economically under-developed country into one of the world's leading industrial powers. Indeed many Italians now claim that Italy has beaten Britain in the international industrial league table. And the major processes of change —industrialisation, urbanisation, mass migration and secularisation— have had profound and long-lasting social and political consequences. The purpose of these essays is to look at various aspects of the patterns of life and politics in Italy today which are largely the result of these changes.

Luisa Quartermaine examines the processes of the social, and especially cultural, transformation which accompanied economic development. In particular, she concentrates on the contribution made by such factors as the dramatic decline in illiteracy, urbanisation and the emergence of the mass media in the creation for the first time in Italy of a uniform, nation-wide mass culture.

Martin Slater traces the course of the post-war process of economic development in Italy, and examines the major effects of this development in the social and, above all, political fields. It is in this context that he locates and explains important, if largely unsuccessful, political experiments like the 'opening to the Left' in the 1960s, and the *compromesso storico* of the 1970s. He ends with a review of the problems which faced the government of Italy's first Socialist Prime Minister, Bettino Craxi, and of the conflicts preceding the 1987 election.

The rise of the Italian steel industry was one of the more spectacular success stories of Italy's 'economic miracle' in the 1950s and 1960s; it also appears to have been a major contributory cause of the massive public debt which burdens the Italian State today. John Eisenhammer examines both the economic context and the politics of the decision-making processes which made continued growth possible in a declining world market, but left the industry in a critical condition. The process of secularisation has had the effect of greatly weakening the influence of the Catholic Church in Italian society as a whole, and in political life in particular. Paul Furlong sets out to analyse the changing role of the Vatican in Italian politics, concentrating on the differing personalities and policies of a succession of occupants of the papal throne. Not least among them is the present Pope, whose Polish background has brought about the most significant change in the Vatican's attitude to Italy since the election of John XXIII in 1958.

The remaining essays are concerned with two phenomena—coalition government and clientelism—which are as characteristic of Italian politics today as they were forty years ago. But coalition-making has undoubtedly become difficult and more tortuous as a result of economic and social changes and the response of politicians and parties to those changes. Geoffrey Pridham offers us a guide to the very complex, not to say labyrinthine, processes whereby a *crisi di governo* finally leads to the formation of yet another *pentapartito* or even a *monocolore* government.

Finally, James Walston focuses on one of the most essential 'lubricants' of the Italian political process—clientelism. Choosing for his case study a very typical environment, Calabria, and using both Christian Democratic and Socialist MPs as examples, he illustrates the crucial role which the distribution of patronage resources plays in the making and unmaking of local elections and of local politicians.

SPEAKING WITH ONE VOICE:

SOCIETY AND MASS MEDIA IN POST-WAR ITALY

Luisa Quartermaine

'ITALY is a strange country' the film director Alberto Lattuada once remarked. 'It is the only country where . . . the head of the Church, a monarch and a dictator can live together and even like each other.'[1] Lattuada was talking about Fascist Italy, but contemporary Italy can be equally baffling. Perhaps this is because its geographical structure and position have given the country a fractured complexity which escapes all definition and the accepted views of Italy have often suffered from gross oversimplification which through inertia or habit have become alarmingly reductive.

Italy is still partly the product of an old tradition that saw the intellectuals grouped together in an élite, and partly the result of the ideological discussions of the late Sixties one of the most lively periods in recent Italian history. Today it offers the same uneasy balance of power of the early Medieval city-states and Renaissance principalities, except that its 'unity' is now achieved through the pressure of the various political parties.[2]

If the importance of a country is determined by its military power, then Italy has been (and still is) a subordinate nation. This was true for the sixteenth-century historians Machiavelli and Guicciardini and has been even more so in recent times. After the events that occurred between 1940 and 1945, for many Italy was totally defeated and with a double stigma, association with Nazism and betrayal of trust. Losing the war dispelled for good the illusion of the strong, compact homogeneous country that Fascism liked to believe it was achieving. Italy's decision-making is now partly dictated by the intrinsic duality between North and South — a duality which the recent industrial revolution has only moderately affected — and partly by outside pressure from the powers that were victorious in the last war. It is a nation with a firm Catholic tradition, but one also strongly attracted towards a lay Communist alternative. From the very beginning of the post-war period, as Giorgio

1

Bocca has argued, the Christian Democrats who came to power felt the need for a strong Communist party whose very presence, as a reaction, would help elicit support for them from the Anglo-Americans and would also help contain pressure from the Vatican. In the same way the Communist party saw the strength of the DC as a guarantee against Soviet attempts to turn the Italian PCI into a tool for their own purposes.[3]

Moreover, in spite of the strong anti-Fascist feeling expressed after the war, Fascism never died entirely. It remained for many a deep-rooted source of memory and remorse; considered as unmitigated evil by some, it was denounced rather than analysed. Anti-Fascism and the myth created by the Resistance, easily charged with emotion by inflamed rhetoric, have been an entrenched part of the institutional framework and have put their stamp on much of post-war Italy's intellectual life, but their validity has begun to be questioned in recent years.

Even factors that from the time of unification should in theory have helped to mould the new nation (the two world-wars, industrialisation, the establishment of a state school system) to some extent worked in the opposite direction. Italy is still characterised by a marked polycentrism, and the cultural differences between regional and social groups, the number of urban centres with their own remote but identifiable ethnic origins, have remained at a level unknown in the rest of Europe.

But where does a province end and a nation begin? What are the boundaries between a dialect and a language? Guido Quazza recognised the problem:

> If one looks at politics only, or at the parties (perhaps without even considering the trade unions), how is it ever possible to understand anything of the change that occured in Italy after the Fifties when 'modernisation' (to use a term which is dearer to the political and social scientists than to historians) has involved 15 million people, from the South to the North, from the country to the towns, from the illiterate to the educated, from a peasant to an industrial culture, and forcibly placed Italy within the world markets.[4]

In studying the cultural transformation of Italy all these factors should be considered, in particular the change that occurred in the pattern of the language used, and the overall effect of education and mass communication. To understand what is happening today we must look at the origin of that cycle of events which covers the last fifty years.

The period from 1943 until 1953 coincided, first of all, with the collapse of Fascism; the political and cultural climate created by the Resistance was in many ways responsible for the new intellectual vitality of the post-war years, with the principal parties, previously involved in the anti-Fascist struggle, strengthened by popular support in a manner completely new to Italian history.

In April 1945, confronted with the disastrous effect of the war and the realisation of the real condition of the country (half of the agricultural industry wiped out, three-quarters of the merchant navy sunk, over 200,000 people roofless in both Turin and Milan, 20 per cent of the living accommodation destroyed in Naples), the decline in patriotism was balanced by the urgent need to reconstruct. This was undertaken with determination, spurred on by a belief that mass prosperity could be brought about by science and technology. The time was ripe for powerful organisations, some private, some State owned, to establish themselves both nationally and internationally. These organisations were mainly concentrated in the North-West of the country; six companies produced almost 93 per cent of the electricity, Finsider had almost total monopoly of the steel industry, Fiat controlled 61 per cent of the car production, and Olivetti had a total monopoly in the office equipment market. To the general pattern of reconstruction Enrico Mattei added his own contribution as head of the new state-owned conglomerate ENI (Ente Nazionale Idrocarburi), soon to become a powerful organisation which, together with Fiat and Pirelli, dictated the financial development of Italy. There is no doubt that the miraculous economic growth brought with it a cultural revolution, even if only in specific sectors. One of these sectors was education.

Culturally Italy was, until the 1950s, still a depressed country with a rural economy (40 per cent of its population worked in agriculture). Illiteracy had indeed decreased by comparison with the calculated 69 per cent of the 1870s, but it remained high at 13 per cent and was, moreover, concentrated in certain areas of the North-East and the South.[5] Italian culture could, at this date, be considered still basically an oral culture, regional and local rather than national, but with the peculiar addition of international elements which the frequent contacts with emigrant communities had introduced. The main mode of expression for these local cultures was dialect. More than any other country in Europe, Italy has for centuries seen the coexistence of several idioms which have reflected the extremely varied ethnic origin of its people. Even today, in the survival of many dialects we can recognise the mark of a long-established regional history. Since the beginning of the twentieth century, and after the standstill of the Fascist period, regional dialects have undergone a substantial change. From being the language most commonly used orally by the majority of people in their social exchanges, they have gradually become the language for only the most informal, private circumstances, often limited to the close circle of relatives and even restricted to the older people in a group.

In the early 1950s only about 24 per cent of the population spoke Italian daily,[6] about 50 per cent spoke the regional dialects, and the others alternated between the two. Out of 19 regions (plus the two provinces under special rule), 15 — with a total of two and a half million people — were directly affected by the presence of a native community speaking a non-Italo-Romance language.[7]

Dialect was for most Italians the live language used for business and social exchange. By the mid-Fifties the cultural transformation resulting from industrialisation and mass migration had begun, but the separation between people who spoke Italian and those who did not acquired a further dimension in the cultural difference between country and town, the peasant environment with its poor school facilities, and the humanistically-oriented education of the town-dwellers.

The Fifties were characterised by an unprecedented interest in educational problems, with all the political parties involved in animated debates sparked off by an inquiry into poverty which the government had launched in 1952 and which drew attention to the connection between illiteracy and unemployment.[8]

The direct result of those debates was a programme of mass education that not only promoted primary schools (for the six- to ten-year olds), but also favoured the introduction of some 2,000 new institutions for specialised professional training. The intention was to look at the problem of education qualitatively as well as quantitatively. These innovations, combined with the introduction in 1962 of compulsory education to the age of fourteen, brought about a remarkable change. Illiteracy dropped to a level of 8 per cent and, more significantly, the pattern of schooling began to move away from the traditional pyramid, large at the base (equivalent to the five years of primary school) and quickly narrowing itself at the secondary and tertiary levels of education.[9]

By the mid-Fifties the numbers of students in secondary education had more than doubled, both in the *medie inferiori* (the ten- to thirteen-year old group), and in the *scuole superiori* (the fourteen- to eighteen-year old group). University students, too, increased by approximately one third (from 200,000 to 300,000), although secondary and tertiary education was still considered a privilege and not a right.

In the same period, after the political defeat of the Left (and of the Communist Party in particular), the general interest of the population shifted away from political involvement towards personal, economic improvement. By the end of the Fifties, 43 million people (36 million more than in 1951) had reached a level of income deemed sufficient to provide relative comfort. Urbanisation on a mass scale and a better standard of living were the two main conditions that promoted both investment in education and better use of the school facilities of the cities. A real race towards education ensued, with the main increase taking place between 1957 and 1962. It was in the latter year that the government took the decision to accelerate the school-building programme, and in three years spent a budget originally allocated for the next ten years. The student population had, by then, increased by one million.

A further dramatic change took place with the introduction, in 1962, of the *scuola media unica*, a unified type of education for all the eleven-to thirteen-year olds, which attempted to eliminate the anachronistic difference between the practical and humanistic orientation of the previous separate *avviamento* and *media*. This was a major event in the history of education in Italy, whose effect was to be clear only in the early Seventies when almost 90 per cent of the eleven-to thirteen-year olds were recorded as regularly attending school (as against a mere 50 per cent in 1959–60). The upward trend in the student population was seen also in the universities, which between 1962–3 and 1975 trebled their students.

What were the consequences of all these changes? The most immediate ones were of a social nature and were positive: an increase in employment, with availability of jobs almost meeting the demand, a better-educated working class with higher standards of life and socially more powerful, an increased number of women holding jobs (about one third of the workforce) and studying at a university (over 40 per cent of the students), more democratic freedom and social mobility between classes. Other consequences were not so positive. The advantages of expansion in education were soon to be measured against imbalances in other sectors, the most significant being the sudden reduction in the labour force in the rural areas and the massive urbanisation and internal migration. (Statistics suggest that between 1959 and 1973 the rural work-force decreased from a total of almost 7 million to just over 2 million.)

If schooling was instrumental in bridging the gap between the social classes and the cultures of the various regions, it also created a deeper gap between the generations. In fact, the changed pattern in education initially affected only the younger generation and was not matched by an adequate policy of adult education. As a result there was soon a younger generation of mainly city-dwellers much better educated than the older, mainly rural one, a different type of divide with potentially serious consequences for the whole fabric of society.

In the Fifties Italian culture was still sharply divided between national aspirations and village traditions, underdeveloped rural areas and industrial cities, a distinction which even the introduction of compulsory military service did not abolish. Italy was still a country in which two thirds of the population did not read books or newspapers;[10] the difference between the *classe colta*, who read books, newspapers and periodicals, and the uneducated, who read only *fotoromanzi*, was still strong. The barrier between *cultura* and *sottocultura* ('high culture' and 'popular culture') signified a division between a progressive and a backward-looking society. But what the school system could not do for the older generation was instead achieved by the mass media of radio, television and the cinema. Radio, or URI (Unione Radiofonica Italiana), was established in Rome in 1924, with the first broadcast being made on 6 October.

After the interlude of EIAR (Ente Italiano Audizioni Radiofoniche) during the Fascist Regime, the present RAI (Radio Audizioni Italiane) began on 26 October 1944 with *Rete azzurra* and *Rete rossa*. In 1951 they became three different and complementary programmes: *Nazionale*, *Secondo* and *Terzo*. Meanwhile the first experimental television show was produced by RAI in Turin in 1949, followed by another in Milan in 1952. It is at this time (March 1952) that the State institution IRI (Istituto per la Ricostruzione Industriale) acquired a major share in the company.

If technically Italy introduced TV rather late (with regular broadcasts starting only in January 1954, Italy came ninth among the countries in Europe), the potential of TV was quickly understood. RAI had, in fact, agreed with the government in 1952 to establish the TV network in three stages, over a period of fourteen years; in practice, this was achieved by January 1957, ten years earlier than planned.

As for radio licences, they had risen from two million in 1948 to well over five million by the early Fifties.[11] An analogous pattern of increase can be found in TV licences, once the medium was introduced. This coincided with the period of the industrial boom, in Italy in particular of domestic appliances. Over one million TV licences were sold between 1954 and 1958, twice that number in 1960, and four million in 1963.[12] Because of the relatively low cost of licences, the subscribers were equally distributed between the regions and the various social classes. According to Giovanni Cesareo the average audience in 1977 was estimated at around 23 million for the programmes between 7.45 p.m. and 9.45 p.m.[13]

The function of TV in the transformation of the country was twofold: it affected the economy directly not only through the sale of the television sets, but also, with the introduction of advertisements, through the sale of industrial products throughout the country; culturally and politically, it gave a new orientation to the use of free time. Moreover, through the simultaneous communication of information and news from various parts of Italy, it strengthened people's sense of belonging to one nation.

> In Italy there is only one daily known in every corner of the country, in the North as in the South, in rich and poor houses alike: it is the TV news. It reaches even the illiterates. This daily is, therefore, the main source of information for the great majority of Italians.[14]

Opinions such as this were not uncommon and to a large extent justified. In spite of Leonardo Sciascia's and Pier Paolo Pasolini's campaigns against TV (or any 'standardised' instrument of mass information) and their stress on the undesirable aspects of the phenomenon, television became *de facto* the main source for shared experience and for models of behaviour. At least 33 per cent of the uneducated adult generation could reach, through TV, a level of general knowledge similar to that given by primary education. Especially significant in this respect were the programmes such as *Non è mai troppo tardi (It is Never Too Late)* that aimed at improving the literacy of older people, particularly in depressed areas.

TV was also the ideal means for the ordinary person to become an actor. The birth of the quiz programmes such as the famous *Lascia o raddoppia (Take it or Double it)*, introducing within the parameters of television the fundamental neo-realist principle of the non-professional protagonist, allowed 'everyman' to enter the television star-system and, in so doing, broke down the mystical division between actor and public; hence the popularity of such programmes. The impact of television has been clearly noticeable in the changes that have affected the use of the spoken language in the last twenty years or so. The difference between those who spoke Italian and those whose only language was dialect often indicated a difference of social class and culture. In the Seventies the percentage of the people who spoke Italian went up from 18 per cent to 25 per cent; at the latest count (in 1984), the number had increased to over 50 per cent. Most Italians are by now aware of belonging to one social system and of sharing what has become a 'national' language. This historic fact has brought with it a number of linked reactions. In particular, through the use made by radio and TV of interviews and live programmes, the barriers between the regional dialects have been reduced; the written language has become more flexible and has often incorporated words and structures of the spoken regional idioms. Dialects, too, have become receptive to the influence of the written

language. What is often seen as careless or degraded use of the once
'unviolated' Italian, is the sign of a new social mix. The 'pure' language
is no longer tied to the classical concept of *otium*, but has become the
language of *negotium*. As Tullio De Mauro said in 1973: 'The Italian
language is no longer Sunday best; it is the everyday overall; it gets
dirtied and abused.[15] There are also new jargons being introduced, such as
the so-called *radiolese* (a kind of supra-regional dialect used primarily by
the large group of young people operating the vast network of private
radio stations in the late Seventies) or the political jargons, such as
sinistrese, of politicians and newspapers.

The greater confidence acquired through the new familiarity with
Italian helped to close the gap in reading habits as well. The years
between 1965 and 1975 witnessed the boom in production and sales of
periodicals. Several publishing houses such as Editori Riuniti, Einaudi, Il
Mulino, La Nuova Italia, and La Scuola, started new types of
publications (for example, *Strumenti Critici, Studi Storici, L'architettura*)
covering a wide range of social and historical interests. In 1963–4
Fratelli Fabbri launched weekly issues of *Dispense*, while in 1965
Mondadori began publishing a series of cheap editions: the weekly and
monthly *Oscar* dedicated to fiction, poetry and theatre, and the
fortnightly *Record* devoted to diaries, biographies and travel.

The possession of a common language not only reduced the shame
once connected with the use of dialects, but on the contrary placed the
dialects in a new perspective; it emphasised the validity of the different
cultures they reflected and stressed the right not to be absorbed into an
anonymous homogeneity.[16]

What television did was to provide a common ground for all; what it
did not do — at least in the early days — was to look critically at the
problems of society and institutions. In spite of the three categories in
which TV programmes were divided (information, culture, entertain-
ment) they all remained essentially a form of evasion and the search for
the common denominator between North and South, the industrial and
the depressed areas, was detrimental to their quality. The presence of
censorship applied by the political party in power (even if often it took
the form of self-applied censorship), the absence until recently of
alternative points of view, the stress on entertaining rather than
informing, all resulted in bland programmes which contributed very little
to political awareness or civic responsibilty. 'Populism' was a real
danger; 'massification' of moral and ideological conformism could well
be the by-product of an ambiguously 'neutral' *cultura dello svago*, which
carefully avoided all controversial issues. It was only at the end of the
cultural unification of the country that the process of differentiation set

in. In TV this coincided with the introduction in 1961 of the *Secondo Canale* and, with it, of an ever-increasing number of debates and documentary investigations presenting alternative points of view. This is particularly significant if compared with the early political organisation of RAI-TV.

The decision taken in the early days by the managerial committee of RAI-TV to opt for one linked programme, to be broadcast simultaneously by the three transmitters of Milan, Turin and Rome, was fundamental not only socially but politically, because it clarified in the eyes of the viewers the position of Rome as the capital city. All the material, in fact, even if produced elsewhere, had to be broadcast from Rome.[17]

This position was reinforced by Filippo Guala, the new *Amministratore Delegato* of RAI-TV, chosen by the Fanfani government, who in 1954 moved the *direzione dei programmi* from Milan to Rome, which remained the pattern for years to come. The move was very likely inspired by the DC, the political party in power, which had been quick to enter the managerial body of RAI-TV and to take advantage of the new medium. Until quite recently it had almost total monopoly of the institution and, in this respect, the history of RAI-TV is political history.[18]

The Left and the Communist party in particular, underestimating the potential of the new medium, preferred originally to distance themselves from it, believing that it represented the late, perhaps more refined, phase of cultural degradation promoted by the bourgeois, consumer society.[19] Even the discussions in the early Seventies about liberalisation of radio and TV were strongly opposed by the Left intelligentsia on the basis that the high costs of the radio, and particularly of TV broadcasting would have required the support of a strong economic entity.[20] This, in turn, would have been difficult to control and could have become an embarrassment. It is basically the same policy that was applied to cinema in which the Left was deeply involved, but only in the film as product, without being concerned in the organisation of the industry.

The strong commitment of the Left to cinema was based on ideological principles such as freedom of expression, investigation of human problems and social conditions, and denunciation of social injustice. In practice this resulted in a strong defence of the neo-realist films (firmly opposed by the government)[21] and of the *cinema d'autore*, with Luchino Visconti and Roberto Rossellini in the forefront.

As late as 1961 Carlo Lizzani could describe the strange apathy that kept the intellectuals working in cinema away from the industry as: 'the most striking phenomenon of non-cooperation between art and industry ever to be experienced in the cinema industry anywhere'.[22]

Yet it is that very barrier between 'art' and 'industry' mentioned by

Lizzani that favoured the realisation of films of uncompromisingly high quality, even if their influence on mass production was negligible. Their 'authors', campaigning for freedom of expression and the right to creativity, fought for independent financial support and, in so doing, retired into a separate, social group of cultural hegemony.

By contrast, the DC had since the late Forties showed a clear pragmatic policy of involvement with the cinema as industry, trying to gain control over markets and distribution. This coincided with the view and the policy of the Church. Remo Branca wrote:

> If the bishops of the whole world could consider the potential offered to any parish, Sunday school or institution by the use of 16mm films, it would be possible to see the miracle of capital and the devil himself coming to the service of God and the Church.
> 1)   One must introduce a stricter attitude and a more widely-spread code of behaviour amongst Catholics towards restricted films.
> 2)   Film production must not be ignored.
> 3)   In our own film production, we must abolish the concepts of capital written off, or given to a charitable organisation. This mistaken policy weakens us in the face of outside propaganda and competition.
> 4)   Wherever possible, through 'Christian funds', so to speak, we must gain access to cinema-halls and distribution networks already in existence.
> 5)   Above all, within the space of 5-7 years we must establish throughout the world between 100,000 and 150,000 cinemas for 16mm films.[23]

In 1949 ACEC (Azione Cattolica Esercenti Cinema) was founded and benefited from particular economic favours such as income tax relief. 'A cinema for every belfry' became the slogan of the parish priest and by 1935, ten years before the economic boom, the number of parish cinemas had reached its peak, with an increase of 1,000 per cent over the post-war years.[24] Most effective was the moralistic campaign which, alongside warnings against the apocalyptic dangers of the new 'monster', saw the organisation of a team of intellectuals, academics, critics, and directors (Diego Fabbri, Remo Branca, Mario Verdone, Giuseppe Flores D'Arcais), who were to offer professional plausibility and expert backing to the cultural, Catholic battle. As Giuseppe Flores D'Arcais wrote in *La Rivista del cinema:* 'Catholic film criticism must be the responsibility of Catholics that is of all-embracing man'.[25] This responsibility was partly taken up by *Cineforum*, a Catholic organisation that acted effectively not only in the selection of films, but much more in their distribution and presentation to an audience that was becoming increasingly aware of the new medium.

Against Catholic censorship (CCC), national censorship, and the local intervention of the *Questura* (Police Headquarters), the lay films had a tough time. Their survival was ensured mainly through key centres, such as the *Centro Sperimentale di Cinematografia*, and specialised periodicals, such as *Bianco e Nero* (promoted by the *Centro*) and *Cinema*. 'Let us defend the art of cinema' was the title of the 1951 declaration, signed by the better-known film directors.[26] The defence took place through a network of cultural organisations which created a more aware audience.[27] Even the most 'difficult' and anti-commercial of films, screened in special cinemas, could find their enthusiastic supporters. Neo-realism had prepared the taste for a cinema that was not afraid to investigate life and to criticise social conditions, and after the short period in the Fifties when the cinema of evasion seemed to override any other interest, the Sixties (which opened with the trio Antonioni, Fellini, Visconti) saw the return to films with a socio-political content. It was the beginning of the so-called *cinema civile* that, through the Sixties and the Seventies, acquired a dimension that television could not (or would not) offer. In spite of various crises and uneven results, the problems connected with 'civic' life—migration, social tension, corruption, speculation and the mafia—were systematically investigated. Alongside the names of well-known film directors (such as Bellocchio, Bertolucci, Olmi, Pasolini, Rosi, Scola, Taviani) some new directors, who had previously worked as militant critics or committed writers (Lino Miccichè, Giuseppe Ferrara, Vittorio De Seta), brought into their films the strength of their ideology and the awareness that the Italian social structure was at breaking point.

Humour has also been an important feature of Italian cinema. It was particularly evident in the comedies of the so-called *realismo rosa* of the Fifties which could display, in their worst examples, a series of vulgar, gratuitous gags, but were, at best, witty representations of human behaviour.

From the few films that were produced in the late Forties, to the 200–250 films of the best years (with an average of 150 films per year), there is no doubt that the culture of Italy has been significantly moulded by the cinema. Although some of it was bad and some insignificant, film became the best channel in which the climate and creative quality of Italian culture could be revealed. Paolo and Vittorio Taviani expressed their clear awareness of the value of the medium:

> What we tried to do was to rediscover that sense of story-telling which goes directly to the heart of things, the way that the great stories have been handed down over the centuries. If we succeeded in this, then the film is what we wanted. And if cinema and television today can assume this traditional role of story-telling, then they will become increasingly the art-form of the future.[28]

This is also proved by the serious cultural approach shown by the major film festivals of Italy, those held in Venice, Taormina, Salsomaggiore and Pesaro, where cultural aspirations and commercial enterprise ensure an effective mechanism of publicity. But each region in Italy has, by now, important film events each year, partly subsidised by the government, partly by the Local Authorities, and also with considerable funds from the major industrialists nearby.[29]

As Umberto Eco has pointed out,[30] an interesting new development that emerged from the mass media was the creation of an instant criticism of those media themselves through the birth of self-supporting newspapers *(Manifesto, Lotta continua, Il quotidiano dei lavoratori)*. The significance of these newspapers was that they showed a new style of writing and a new way of presenting the news (including news disregarded by the traditional press). This happened at the crucial time of the students' revolt in 1968, which was in itself a phenomenon of mass proportions.

Increased politicisation was seen also among intellectuals, especially in those who had emerged from the so-called *Gruppo '63*. Their interests, based on less literary and increasingly more social and political issues, were documented in a short-lived journal *Quindici* (1967–69), that took the name from the number of its founding members (among whom was Umberto Eco). It became for a time a popular forum for new ideas. In particular, in the light of the dramatic national and international events, it discussed the role of intellectuals in relation to the students' movement and to society in general.

It is extremely difficult to analyse the complex and often contradictory phenomenon of the *contestazione*. It is certainly true that the uncritical enthusiasm of the early days of reconstruction brought prosperity, but with it came major problems. Society by the mid–Sixties had changed; the sprawling industrial cities of the North had multiplied their ghettoes, but could neither contain demands nor satisfy expectations. They became city-dormitories which eventually produced the violence of the Seventies and fostered terrorism. With the Seventies we enter the present period of social instability and social recrimination which neither the government, nor the traditional institution of the Church has been able to contain. Schools, universities and major industries such as Fiat became arenas for a strategy of tension. Within the national union of students (UNURI) several political groups came in existence: the Left was represented by UGI (Unione Goliardica Italiana), the most active of the groups; the Liberals by AGI (Associazione Goliardica Italiana); the Christian-Democrats by *Intesa;* the Right by FUAN (Fronte Universitario di Azione Nazionale).

One of the first episodes of students' unrest, in February 1962, was the seizure of 'La Sapienza', the Great Hall of Pisa University. This happened during the visit of the then Minister of Education, Luigi Gui, who was to preside over a meeting of Vice Chancellors. The students' action was intended as a clear protest against the inadequacies of the education system and against the structure of the universities in particular. Similar action was taken in other parts of Italy, particularly in Rome, Milan, Turin and Venice and had repercussions in the whole field of labour during the so-called *autunno caldo* (hot autumn). In Milan the unrest reached the Catholic University, where the students' movement had among its activists Michelangelo Spada, the future leader of *Lotta Continua*. The centre which was to become the most controversial, however, was the newly-established Faculty of Sociology at Trento University. Founded by the local Christian-Democrat Flaminio Piccoli, whose intention was to bring new life to the quiet city, it soon attracted (together with prestigious academics) subversive, radical groups of students whose names later became associated with terrorist movements (Marco Boato, Mauro Rostagno, Renato Curcio, Margherita Cagol). Renato Curcio, one of the founders of the Red Brigades, introduced the idea of a 'negative university' on the model of the Berlin *Kritische Universität*.

If we look at the evolution of the Left terrorist movement, we can distinguish at least five main groups: the group of students from Trento, who soon moved to the more central and active Milan; the Communists from Reggio Emilia, with Alberto Franceschini; the followers of Giangiacomo Feltrinelli, the Milanese publisher, founder of the deservedly famous *Istituto per la storia del movimento operario* (he was to be killed on an electricity pylon while supposedly planting explosives); the two political associations of *Potere Operaio* and *Lotta Continua*. The best organised, however, and also the most violent group to emerge in the late Seventies was *Autonomia Operaia*, which included among its members people from different backgrounds and had in Toni Negri, a professor in the Faculty of Political Science at Padua University, its intellectual theoretician. The causes of the revolt were many and complex. What they have in common was a basic mistrust of the ruling class, an awareness of the lack of leadership and the prospect of little change. The tension among the extreme-Left was further increased by the adoption of a policy of cooperation with the government (the famous *compromesso storico*) that the PCI leader, Enrico Berlinguer, had promoted since 1973. Toni Negri himself was arrested under the acusation of involvement in the kidnapping and death of Aldo Moro, the one politician who might have brought about the *compromesso storico*.

The terrorism of the extreme-Right was equally violent, but has received less attention from contemporary commentators, and its strength has probably been underestimated. It often smacked of neo-Fascism and showed nostalgia for strong values and a Eurocentric, imperialistic Europe. It had links with the mafia and with the Fascist *legionari* of the Salò Republic, hence the prominence given to the personality of Prince Junio Valerio Borghese, who had been the Commander of the famous (some would say infamous) *Decima Mas* during the Salò Regime. One of the supporters of right-wing terrorism was Franco Freda, the man accused of the 1969 Piazza Fontana outrage in Milan. There are also strong suspicions that the ruling class might have been implicated in the activities of the so-called *trame nere* and that this 'black terrorism' might have infiltrated the State Secret Service. It has been calculated that the number of neo-Fascist groups that in one way or another have been supportive of violent actions are more than 60. The most important are *Avanguardia Nazionale* (with its leader Stefano Delle Chiaie), and *Ordine Nuovo*, which promulgates a journal by the same name, a periodical called *Voi Europa* and a bulletin on the Third World, *Eurafrica*. The bombs exploded in Piazza della Loggia, Brescia (May 1974), on the train *Italicus* (August 1974), at Bologna station (Summer 1980), and on the Naples-Milan express train (December 1984) are possible examples of their destructive power. The philosophy of *Nuova Destra*, a new movement born in 1977, has been the subject of a recent investigation, the results of which were discussed at an international conference in Turin (June 1984). It seems to count already 3–4,000 members, equally distributed throughout Italy, and is closely connected with the most extreme forms of neo-Fascism. It finds inspiration, beyond Gentile and Mussolini, in the writing of Soffici, Papini or in the German-inspired ultra-Fascism of Julius Evola; it appears to have links with the French *Nouvelle Droite* and similar organisations in Germany and Great Britain. The common ideology of such movements can be summed up in the following attitudes: an anti-democratic view of the world, a nostalgia for past hierarchical systems of law and order, the accepted concept of inequality and the 'need' for a cultural hegemony.[31] This is history which is still being written, but if the false simplicity of such neo-Fascist appeals continues to attract willing hands to their cause, the strength and sincerity of popular revulsion at their outrages bears witness to the continuing diversity of modern Italian life.

NOTES

1 Interview published in *Nuovi materiali sul cinema italiano*, 1929–1943, 2 vols, Mostra Internazionale del Nuovo Cinema, Roma, 1976, p. 125.

2 'The main role of DC is the same that the Church had in the Middle Ages. It is an unstable entity, uncertain between favouring the North or the South. . . . The Communist opposition has the same double nature of the Republic of Venice. . . . The Socialist party is not unlike the duchy of Milan, full of potential, but unable to establish its own superiority. . . . The Republican party . . . is like the beautiful city of Florence . . . the Liberals like Genoa . . . and finally the Right, like the *reame*, the kingdom of the South, it can never develop any modern, coherent policies, but is nevertheless an invisible, stabilizing force within the system'. (L. Garruccio, *Italia senza eroi*, Rusconi, Milano, 1980, p. 52. My translation here and in the following passages.)

3 G. Bocca, *Storia della Repubblica Italiana dalla caduta del Fascismo a oggi*, Rizzoli, Milano, 1982, p. 7 ff.

4 G. Quazza, 'L'Italia negli ultimi trent'anni', in *Rassegna critica degli studi, Atti del seminario promosso dal Consiglio Regionale della Toscana*, Il Mulino, Bologna, 1978, pp. 48–50.

5 P. Luzzatto-Fegiz, *Il volto sconosciuto dell'Italia*, sec. serie, Giuffré, Milano, 1966, p. 1339 ff.

6 Tullio De Mauro believes that the more realistic figure is closer to 18 per cent. Cf. T. De Mauro, 'La cultura', in AAVV, *Dal 68 a oggi: come siamo e come eravamo*, Laterza, Bari, p. 199.

7 T. De Mauro, *L'Italia delle Italie*, Nuova Guaraldi, Firenze, 1979, p. 35.

8 G. Ricuperati, 'Scuola e movimento degli studenti' in *Italia Contemporanea 1945–1975*, Einaudi, Torino, 1976, p. 438.

9 Cf. *Sviluppo dell'istruzione*, Ufficio Studi Documentazione e Programmazione del Ministero della Pubblica Istruzione, Roma, 1963.

10 According to statistics issued by ISTAT in 1959, 41 per cent of Italian families read nothing and only 8 per cent read books.

11 F. Alberoni, 'Presenza della TV in Italia', in *Televisione e vita italiana 1954–1966*, ERI, Torino, 1968, p. 18.

12 Cf. *Annuario RAI*, ERI, Torino, 1964, p. 451. Interesting statistical facts can be found in *Intellettuali e TV negli anni 50*, ed. by F. Pinto, Savelli, Roma, 1977.

13 G. Cesareo, 'L'avvento della televisione e il cinema negli anni cinquanta', in *Il cinema italiano degli anni 50*, Marsilio Editori, Venezia, 1979, pp. 340–362.

14 N. Adelfi, 'Prefazione' to G. Mottana, *Il mestiere del giornalista*, Guido Miano Ed., 1967, p. 9.

15 T. De Mauro, 'La cultura', in Dal 68 a oggi . . . op. cit. p. 202. Also on the same subject, cf. M. Dardano, *Il linguaggio dei giornali*, Laterza, Roma-Bari, 1973.

16 This is an issue which is still very much debated in schools and has not yet been solved satisfactorily. It was at the heart of the accusation of the pupils of Don Milani's famous *Scuola Barbiana*. Cf. L. Renzi, M. A. Cortelazzo, *La lingua italiana oggi: un problema scolastico e sociale*, Il Mulino, Bologna, 1977.

17 The alternative would have been to have different programmes for different parts of Italy. It is an interesting piece of legislation, particularly if compared with the troubles that, in late October 1984, afflicted the private TV networks of *Canale 5*, *Italia 1* and *Retequattro* owned by Berlusconi. The decision of three magistrates to stop the programmes in the areas of Lazio, Piedmont and Abruzzo was apparently taken on the basis that it was illegal for these private networks to broadcast nationally, since this was a prerogative of RAI (cf. *Corriere della sera*, Mercoledì, 17 ottobre 1984, p. 1).

18 G. Cesareo, 'L'avvento della televisione e il cinema degli anni 50', op. cit.

19 F. Pinto, 'La nascita della TV e l'ideologia del rifiuto', in *Il cinema italiano degli anni 50*, op. cit., pp. 363–372.

20 The development of the Japanese electronics industry and the ambiguity of the Italian law favoured the appearance of private radios and the intervention in their organisation of left-wing intellectuals. Stations appeared in hundreds everywhere, even in the most remote villages.

21 G. Andreotti's attitude to neo-realist films is well-known: 'Se nel mondo si sarà indotti erroneamente a ritenere che quella di *Umberto D* è l'Italia della metà del ventesimo secolo, De Sica avrà reso un pessimo servizio alla patria' (quoted in D. Bartoli, *Gli anni della tempesta. Alle radici del malessere italiano*, Editoriale Nuova, Milano, 1981, p. 39). The opinion of Sen. Tupini is even stronger: 'questo sistema della ricerca di soggetti malsani e scandalosi deve cessare . . . a partire da questo momento sarò severissimo in materia di censura' (ibid., p. 39).

22 C. Lizzani, *Storia del Cinema Italiano 1895–1961*, Parenti, Firenze, 1961, p. 40.

23 R. Branca, 'Nuovi orientamenti di fronte al cinematografo', in *L'Osservatore Romano*, 21 aprile '49.

24 G. Brunetta, 'Cattolici e cinema' in *Il cinema degli anni 50*, op. cit., p. 305.

25 Ibid., p. 309.

26 The names were: Antonioni, Blasetti, Camerini, Chiarini, Comencini, De Santis, De Sica, Emmer, Germi, Lattuada, Puccini, Rossellini, Solaroli, Vergano, Visconti, Zampa. Cf. V. Tosi, 'I circoli del cinema e l'organizzazione del pubblico', in *Il cinema italiano degli anni 50*, op. cit., p. 322.

27 Some were rivals, some worked together. Among the best known were: the Associazione Culturale Cinematografica Italiana (ACCI), first established in 1944, it became the *Circolo Romano del Cinema*; the *Federazione Italiana dei Circoli del Cinema* (FICC), in 1953 it counted already over 50,000 members; its two rival groups were: *Unione Italiana Circoli del Cinema* (UICC) and the *Azione cinema libero*, which, small in number but prestigious, worked in cooperation with the Italian association for the freedom of culture (whose president was Ignazio Silone). There were also several *Centri Universitari Cinematografici*, and the *Amici del cinema*. Most of these associations later on joined the *Associazione Nazionale Autori Cinematografici* (ANAC). Cf. V. Tosi, ibid., pp. 334–340.

28 Cf. interview with the Taviani brothers, *South Bank Show*, ITV, Sunday 28 November 1984.

29 Cf. Don Ranvaud, 'Italian Festivals', in *Framework*, no 21, Summer 1983, p. 55.

30 U. Eco, 'New Developments in the Mass Media of Contemporary Italy', *Altro Polo*, 1983, p. 115.

31 Cf. *La Stampa*, sabato 2 giugno 1984, p. 3.

ITALY'S CHANGING POLITICAL ECONOMY

Martin Slater

1. INTRODUCTION: ITALIAN POLITICAL ECONOMY IN THE 1980s

By early 1987, many observers of the Italian scene were proclaiming the dawn of a new era of polictical stability and economic growth. Few would have hazarded such a prediction just four years earlier. In fact the June 1983 elections appeared to leave the Italian political system in considerable disarray. The Christian Democrats, long the dominant party of government, lost a substantial proportion of their vote to junior partners in the Centre coalition. To the decline in their moral authority (a result of corruption scandals in the late 1970s and early 1980s) was added a decline in their political authority. The Socialists, the leading force among the junior coalition partners, were quick to seize the initiative. Within two months, Bettino Craxi, leader of the Socialist Party, had become Prime Minister and presented his administration's programme in parliament.

A close examination of the new government suggested that little had really changed. Like many previous ones, it was a coalition of Christian Democrats, Socialists, Republicans, Social Democrats, and Liberals. The Christian Democrats continued to hold a majority of cabinet positions, and nearly all the most important ministries. Further, the government's programme had clearly been dictated by the Christian Democrats. Emphasising the emplacement of Cruise missiles in Sicily, and the intention to control public spending and wage increases, it was decidedly conservative in tone. The Christian Democrats were not entirely happy about giving up the premiership, which, until 1981, they had regarded as theirs by right. However, they felt confident that within a couple of years, the office would be theirs once again. Craxi, they reasoned, would soon come unstuck on the thorny economic problems facing the nation. Let him take responsibility for the unpopular decisions that would have to be taken. In addition, support for Craxi's premiership now, would create an obligation of Socialist support for a future Christian Democrat premiership.

Such reasoning could not easily be faulted at the time. Certainly few were optimistic about Italy's economic prospects. The golden years of the 1950s and 1960s appeared to be ended for good. World recession in the 1970s coincided with increasing militance and unity of the trade-union movement, on the one hand, and increasing fragmentation of the party system, on the other hand. Economic and political mismanagement characterised this period. It led inevitably to slow and uneven growth, soaring inflation, increasing unemployment, and a growing public sector deficit. The experience of the early 1980s suggested there was to be no let-up to this pattern. During the first three years of the 1980s, Italy's economic performance was, if anything, worse than before. Gross national product declined in each year from 1981 to 1983, but inflation remained in double figures, while unemployment increased, and the public sector deficit rose to around 15% of gross national product.

Against this background, the Craxi government not only managed to survive, but became the longest serving government of post-war Italian history. Its forty three months in office, until March 1987, were twice as long as any previous government. Craxi's success has still to be properly analysed. He was no doubt fortunate in that his tenure of office coincided with some economic good fortune. In his first year of office, the economy grew by 2.8% in response to increased world demand. Growth rates have since remained between 2% and 3%. Inflation was brought down to single figures within a year, and has continued to decline to its current level of 4%. At least part of the decline in inflation is attributable to the fall in oil prices and the decline of the dollar relative to the lira in 1985. This fall substantially reduced the cost of energy, most of which is imported.

In terms of policies, the government kept its promise to reduce wage costs by passing legistlation to limit the automatic index linking of wage increases. But less progress was made in cutting the public sector deficit, which still stands around 12% of gross national product. Craxi's achievement was not so much in making the hard decisions about cutting public expenditure (the improvement in the economy in any case made these decisions less pressing), but more in giving the appearance of doing so. He created around him a aura of *decisionismo* (decisiveness), contrasting sharply with the lack of decisiveness of previous regimes. In addtion, he raised Italy's profile abroad, and helped to restore national pride by taking firm and independent foreign policy stances. Most of all, he proved remarkably obdurate. Providing a sense of purpose and stability to the Italian government that had for so long been lacking, the

Christain Democrats could find no good excuse for removing him from office. Certainly such a move would have been unpopular with many of Italy's leading industrialists who had felt the economic benefits of political stability.

By the beginning of 1987, Italians might have felt justified in believing that a fundamental change had taken place in their economic and political systems. The economy and stockmarket were booming. The lira was increasing in value against both the dollar and sterling. With revisions of statistics of the gross domestic product to include the unofficial economy, Italians could now proclaim that theirs was the world's fifth largest economy, having overtaken the United Kingdom. The next target was France. On the political front, it became possible to believe that the unstable coalitions were a thing of the past. The Italian government appeared stable and effective, and was an authoritative voice in world affairs.

By March 1987, this happy state of affairs was at an end as far as stable and effective government was concerned. In truth, the cracks within the governing coalition had been visible for quite some time. The Christian Democrats felt they had supported Craxi long enough. Now it was his turn to cede the premier's office to a Christian Democrat, and play a supporting role. Despite initial intimations to the contrary to appease the Christian Democrats, it finally became clear that Craxi had no intention of playing a supporting role. Thus the Christian Democrats withdrew their support precipitating early elections in June 1987. Amintore Fanfani returned as caretaker Prime Minister, seeming to indicate a reversion to the previous style and practice of government domination by an aging elite of Christian Democrats. Fanfani had first risen to prominence in the late 1940s, and was already leading the government in the 1950s.

On the surface, the 1987 election appeared to offer voters the choice between the old style of politics and the new. But the election results alone cannot determine the course to be followed. Nor is the choice so stark. Important changes have already occurred which will prevent any return to the system of the 1950s and 1960s. Such changes should not be surprising, considering the enormous socio-economic transformations of the post-war era.

Over the past thirty-five years, Italy has changed from a largely rural, traditional economy to become one of the world's leading industrial nations. The changes have not been spread evenly over the national territory. Parts of Italy, particularly in the South, remain chronically underdeveloped. Other regions, mainly in the North, have experienced remarkable growth. Italy is a land of sharp contrasts, and also of deep social divisions, which have not facilitated the business of government. These contrasts are reflected in the political system, not just by deep ideological divisions, but also by fundamental differences in political relations. Clientelistic patterns of political relationships predominate in the South, while social group relationships predominate in the North. One of the principal ambiguities in the Italian political system is that political power in the post-war era has been concentrated in the hands of a party, the Christian Democrats, that relies heavily on the preservation of clientelistic relations. Thus, despite massive socio-economic change, it seemed that the political system continued much as before. The rise of the Communist Party in the 1970s and lay Centre parties in the 1980s, led by the Socialist Party, challenges the old assumptions.

Two developments are responsible for this change. First, as might be expected, the socio-economic changes that have occurred are increasingly seeping through into the political system. Traditional loyalties have broken down and a process of secularisation has taken place. People's expectations about the political system have also changed. Since the late 1960s, more demands have been made upon the political system, and by many more people than was previously the case. In the terminology of some political scientists, the system has become 'overloaded'.[1] The catalyst of change was the 'hot autumn' of 1969 which marked the rise of a powerful and vociferous workers' movement. At that time, and in the years since, new forms of political participation have developed. Some have been spontaneous, such as the councils in factories (workers' councils) and urban communities (zonal councils). Others have been instituted by the government in response to popular pressure (regional government, for instance). These new institutions have all become channels for the mediation of popular demands. So, too, has the use of the referendum which was resurrected by interest groups and the small Radical Party during the 1970s. Where the channels of mediation have not proved effective, popular protest has taken place on the streets. An ugly side to this protest has been the development of terrorist organisations of both Left and Right, which have been active since 1969. Faced with an explosion of demands, on a vastly expanded terrain of participation, and with declining support for coalitions of the Centre, the political system was long incapable of an effective response. As the country became more ungovernable, the political system has lurched from crisis to crisis. For many, then, the last four years have been the light at the end of the tunnel.

The second development which affected the political system, eroding the power of the parties of government, is partly a product of the first. As more demands were made upon the political system, fewer were satisfied. The economic problems of the 1970s were, to some extent, induced by this excess of demands. High rates of inflation and a growing public sector deficit were symptoms of economic and political mismanagement. As growth declined, the government was faced with hard decisions involving economic austerity. Such conditions have strained to the utmost a system that relies on political patronage. Clientelism works so long as favours can be distributed. But it, too, is subject to its own inflationary pressures.[2]

In the following sections, I shall examine these themes in greater depth, looking, first, at the nature of Italy's socio-economic transformation; and second, at the way the political system has responded. By way of conclusion, I shall examine the major problems of economic management facing the Italian government in the 1980s.

2. SOCIO-ECONOMIC TRANSFORMATION

Industrialisation came relatively late to Italy, compared to some other European nations. Unification had only been achieved in 1861, so it was not till the late nineteenth century that the infrastructure was in place that allowed the development of national markets. Two factors affected the pattern of industrialisation. First, unification had been imposed by the northern state of Piedmont. The South suffered accordingly. The breaking down of trade barriers weakened the South's nascent industries. In addition, the South had to bear the Piedmontese debt, and was saddled with disproportionately high taxes. With these impositions, and far from the growing markets of Northern Europe, the South languished economically compared to the North.[3] Second, Italy had few natural resources of her own. The industries that thrived were small-scale and technologically backward. The textile industry was a typical example. Heavy industry developed on a limited scale in the northern industrial triangle of Genoa, Milan, and Turin. There was no great concentration of working class power. As for the bourgeoisie, it was numerous but lacking in political muscle.

From 1870–1913, the annual rate of growth of total output was 1.4%; from 1913–50, it was 1.3%.[4] The two world wars, twenty years of Fascism, and the depression of the 1930s, all combined to limit Italy's economic development. One lasting effect of Fascism, however, is the presence of a large nationalised sector in the Italian economy. In 1936, the bankruptcy of many of Italy's larger industries, and of the banks who were their creditors, had provoked widespread nationalisations.

By 1950, despite Marshall Aid and some years of economic recovery, the Italian economy was still in a backward state. Unemployment stood

at 10.8%. Hidden unemployment and underemployment were exten-
sive. Agriculture, with 40.8% of the labour force, was the major
economic activity. Industry accounted for 31.8% of the labour force.
The 1951 Census showed that despite the high numbers working in
agriculture, it produced only 23.5% of gross national product; industry
produced 33.7%. These national figures mask the fact that in terms of
economic development the South lagged far behind the North. It had
never recovered from its early economic setbacks.

From the 1950s onwards, Italy's economy was progressively transformed. By 1960, the level of unemployment had fallen to around 3%,
comparable to northern European economies that had enjoyed full
employment since the late 1940s.[5] Between 1950 and 1960, the average
annual rate of growth of total output was 5.9 per cent. From 1956–61,
it was 6.9 per cent. The years from 1958 to 1962 became popularly
known as the years of the 'economic miracle'; during this period, annual
growth rates remained above 6 per cent and touched 8.3 per cent in
1961, among the highest in Europe.[6] Though it never again reached the
peaks of this period, growth continued to be high and smooth right up till
the oil price crisis of the early 1970s. From 1960 to 1970, the average
rate of growth was 5.7 per cent. There were certainly periods of
recession interspersed with the periods of boom, but recession did not
mean economic decline, it merely meant a slowing in the rate of
economic growth. Only once, from 1950 to 1970, did the rate of growth
slip below 3 per cent, when it fell to 2.9 per cent in 1963.[7] Average
annual inflation during the 1950s was only 3.9%.

The 1970s saw a more variable economic performance. The average
growth rate for the decade 1970–1980 was a respectable 3.1%. But, for
the first time in 1974 the economy declined by 3.6%. Periods of strong
recovery have been punctuated by further periods of decline. In addition,
unemployment, inflation, and a burgeoning budget deficit became
serious problems. Between 1970–75, industrial employment grew by
0.5% per annum, but between 1975–80, the figure decline to only
0.1%. Average annual inflation was 11.4% from 1970–75, and
16.8% from 1975–80.[8]

Economic stagnation brought even more misery to the early 1980s. In
1981, gross domestic product increased by only 0.2%. In 1982 and
1983, it declined by 0.5% and 0.2% respectively. Inflation, failing to
respond to recession, continued apace, with an annual average of 13.8%
between 1980–85. Industrial employment decreased by 2.3% annually
over the same period.[9] By 1984, the public sector deficit had soared
above Lit. 100,000 billion (around 15% of gross domestic product), and
the balance of payments was in serious deficit.[10]

By 1984, as noted earlier, the economy began to improve steadily. Estimates for 1987 are a growth rate of 3%, inflation of 4%, and a strong surplus on the balance of payments.[11] The public sector deficit, however, is stubbornly resisting attempts at reduction, while unemployment stands at over two million, or 11.6% of the work-force, and is on an upward trend.

There are various interpretations of Italy's rapid economic growth during the 1950s and 1960s. Some analysts have emphasised the importance of the expansion of aggregate demand.[12] Certainly, internal demand grew during the 1950s, so, too, did international demand. In 1958, Italy had become a founding member of the European Economic Community. Far from killing off Italy's young industries, the breaking down of industrial trade barriers provided the necessary markets. Other observers have given more weight to labour supply as an enabling factor of economic growth.[13] Unemployment had remained high during the 1960s, and the southern part of the country was, in any case, a vast reservoir of labour that was flexible with regard to location and type of work. Both the expansion of demand and the existence of labour reserves were no doubt important to Italy's economic development. What concerns us most, however, is the social impact of rapid growth.

The first effect of economic growth was the change in the country's occupational structure. By 1961, the proportion of the workforce employed in agriculture had declined to 29.7 per cent (40.8 per cent in 1950); by 1971, it was 18.4 per cent; and by 1981, 12.8 per cent. The mass exodus from agriculture was matched by the growth of employment in the industrial and service sectors. The proportion of the workforce employed in industry increased to 38.8 per cent by 1971 (33.7 per cent in 1950), declining to 36.4 per cent in 1981. The proportion employed in the service sector increased more dramatically, rising continuously from 27.4 per cent in 1950 to 50.8 per cent in 1981.[14] The expansion of service sector employment, unlike industrial employment, has not been upset by the economic difficulties of the 1970s. The reasons lie partly in the fact that it is a catch-all category. It groups together such disparate categories as bankers and domestic servants. It also includes public administration, which has not suffered the cutbacks of the other sectors. The proportion of the workforce employed in public administration has grown continuously from 8.2 per cent in 1961 to 14.5 per cent in 1981.

As the occupational structure has changed, so too has the employment status of the workforce. In 1961, 40.2 per cent of the workforce had been self-employed. By 1981, it had declined to 28.5 per cent. This figure is still high compared to, say, Britain, where only 7.7 per cent of the workforce is self-employed.[15] It reflects the early pattern of industrialisation in Italy, which gave rise to a numerous middle class. The continued existence of what might be termed a large petty bourgeoisie has had important political consequences in Italy. Nonetheless, there is no disputing that a decline of the self-employed, and the corresponding rise in the proportion of dependent employees, constitutes a change in the balance of the Italian class structure. When seen together with changes in the occupational structure, a society characterised by self-employment and a largely agricultural workforce can be said to have changed into one in which the industrial and service sectors predominate, and in which most workers are dependent employees.

The significance of these changes cannot be fully understood without looking at the territorial dimension. Economic growth has been overwhelmingly concentrated in the North-Western and Eastern parts of the country. The South has continued to lag behind all the other regions. Between 1951 and 1960, income in the South rose by 80.4 per cent. But, in the rest of the country, it rose by 98.7 per cent.[16] Thus, differentials increased. The South, though holding its own since 1960 has failed to catch up with the North and the latest indications are that it is beginning to slip further behind. Percentage differentials in living standards have remained the same, but absolute differentials have necessarily increased. In 1970, the South, with 35.2 per cent of the population, produced 23.4 per cent of the wealth; in 1980, with 35.6 per cent it produced 23.9 per cent.[17] On a whole host of socio-economic indicators, the South remains underdeveloped. In 1981, agricultural employment in the South was 22.6 per cent of the labour force, compared to 9.3 per cent in the rest of the country, and 6.6 per cent in the industrial North-West. Industrial employment was 27.4 per cent in the South, and 47.7 per cent in the North-West. The service sector, with 50 per cent of the Southern labour force, compared to 45.7 per cent in the North- West, should not be taken as an indication of economic development.[18] Rather, it reflects the over inflated size of this sector which is typical of many Third World economies. In terms of activity rates, in 1981, only 36 per cent of the South's population was active in the labour market, compared to 42.6 per cent in the rest of the country. Of this southern labour force, 12.2 per cent was unemployed, compared to 6.7 per cent elsewhere. (These unemployment figures exclude the numbers working short-time, the so-called *cassa integrazione*.)[19] By 1987, the seriousness of the unemployment in the South was illustrated by the fact that over 30% of the under 30s in Sicily and Calabria were unemployed.

The continued underdevelopment of the South has not simply been the result of government neglect. It is true that development in Italy has not been 'managed' by the State. Despite the presence of a large State industrial sector, development occurred in the most unplanned, *laissez faire* manner. In the case of the South, however, a fund for development, the *Cassa per il Mezzogiorno*, was set up in 1950. For the first few years, most of the funds were channelled into land reform and reclamation projects, which were seen as a prerequisite for industrialisation. Later policies, continuing up to the 1980s, have focused on the provision of infrastructure and providing incentives for industrial development. In addition, from 1957, IRI and ENI, the State-holding companies of the nationalised sector, were obliged to put 60 per cent of new plant investment in the South.[20] Neither the agricultural nor the industrial policies have fulfilled expectations; the land reform policies, for instance, put unqualified farmers with no market knowledge on to relatively unproductive land. The industrial policies have led to the construction of large plants, such as oil refineries in Sicily and steel works in Taranto and Naples. These have provided relatively few employment opportunities since they are capital intensive. In addition, they have provided very little stimulus to the local economies. Overall, not enough funds were provided to allow the South to catch up with the North, and those that were provided were not spent in the wisest manner. Today, the large public sector industries in the South face a particularly severe crisis. As the Italian government grappled with the problems of controlling public sector spending, it has had to face the problem of what to do with its industrial investments in the South. Many plants have been closed down. Such developments have caused additional hardship in the short-term, with no long-term solution in sight. Aggravating matters, the *Cassa per il Mezzogiorno* became bankrupt and was finally wound up in 1984.

The lack of economic opportunities in the South has resulted in massive emigration. Though the southern population has grown at the same rate as that of the rest of the country (owing to a higher rate of natural increase), it is estimated that about five million Southerners have emigrated during the post-war era. Between 1951 and 1976, net emigration from the South was 4.1 million.[21] Southern emigration is by no means a recent phenomenon. What has changed is the destination of emigrants. Before the First World War, millions emigrated to the Americas (more than 800,000 in 1913 alone). Fascism and the world wars interrupted emigration. When it resumed in the late 1940s, France and other industrial regions of Northern Europe became a popular destination. They remained so during the 1950s and 1960s. By the late 1950s, however, economic development in the North-West was beginning to give rise to significant internal migration.[22] Having exhausted their local labour markets, northern industries were increasingly turning to the labour reserves of Southern Italy. In Milan, for instance, almost 100,000 migrants were arriving every year by the late 1950s and early 1960s. From 1961 to 1971, net immigration to Milan was 470,828. In 1956, about one third of these migrants had come from the South, the remainder from the surrounding provinces. By 1970, the South accounted for over 90 per cent of net immigration.[23]

For the South, mass emigration meant the loss of some of the most active and qualified members of the labour force. The very poor, the old, the infirm, and the very young did not migrate. As a result, many southern villages have disproportionate numbers of old people and children, while those of working age have left. In the poorest areas, agricultural lands have been abandoned. It is a debatable point whether emigration of this kind hinders or aids development.[24] One effect of migration is that it has provided a safety valve for the political system. Rural protest is a phenomenon of the past. Violent outbursts in the South have been far more common in the towns and cities where rural migrants have settled in the hope of finding employment. A lack of job opportunities has meant that most of the migrants have been confined to the level of a sub-proletariat, swelling the ranks of an already over-inflated service sector, prone to the persuasion of neo-Fascist groups.

Within the northern industrial regions, southern migrants moved into the burgeoning industrial sector. Typically, they found jobs initially in the more technologically backward sectors of the economy. Lutz notes that between 1950 and 1959, non-agricultural employment absorbed some two million persons, yet only 120,000 were absorbed by the advanced sectors of industry.[25] By the early 1960s, migrants had begun to move into the advanced sector, such as the automobile industry. In these industries, they filled the low-skilled jobs on the assembly-lines. The nature of this work, combined with the archaic and authoritarian system of industrial relations in Italian industry, provided the most alienating work conditions. In addition, within the urban community, the southern migrants suffered social ostracism as well as social deprivation. Confined to the peripheral zones of the city, they faced poor housing conditions and inadequate social infrastructure, including transport and schools.

By 1963, the tightening of the labour market allowed migrants and other members of the working class in Northern Italy to express their demands with more force than usual. The strikes that hit northern industry in that year were met with significant wage increases. At the same time, the Socialists entered the governing coalition. These wage increases were a set-back for the relatively labour intensive Italian economy. International competitivity suffered, and an austerity programme was soon initiated by the new Centre-Left government. It was not till the late 1960s, following economic revival and a further tightening of the labour market, that conditions were once again ripe for the growth of popular protest. In 1968, a series of wildcat strikes hit major industrial firms in the North. In 1969, the metal workers, striking for a new national contract, virtually brought the economy to a halt. This period, known as the 'hot autumn', acted as a catalyst for political change. The protest movement bypassed the traditional mediators of protest, the left-wing political parties and the trade-unions. In this sense, it was very much a grass-roots movement. The unions during the 1950s and 1960s had been weak, isolated, and ideologically divided. They were ineffective negotiators on the shop floor, compared to the workers' councils which sprang up spontaneously in many factories. The demands of the northern working class in these conflicts focused not just on salaries, but also on the nature of work in the factory, the desire to control the type and location of industrial investment, and also on broader social demands. They reflected the exigencies of a socially isolated and alienated immigrant proletariat.[26]

Northern industry was obliged to meet many of the workforce's demands, adding significantly to their costs. Over the next few years, strike activity continued at an intense level. By 1970, the unions had regained control of the movement. But in order to do so they had to put aside many of their ideological differences (the three main union confederations are organised along party/ideological lines), accept the new structures of representation (the workers' councils) that had replaced their own structures in the workplace, and lead the working class in their campaign for economic and social reform. Under these circumstances, the Centre coalitions of the 1970s were put under severe strain, and pressured into concessions that, as it turned out, they could ill afford to make. The major example was the *scala mobile*, the sliding scale under which wage increases are paid. This scale was instituted in 1975 as a result of a tripartite agreement between unions, government, and employees. The system, disproportionately rewarding the lower paid, linked wage increases to an agreed cost of living index. It came to be seen as one of the major elements fuelling the high inflation of recent years, and was finally subjected to far-reaching reforms in 1983 and 1984.

The strength of the workers' movement during the 1970s also gave rise to the gradual diffusion of economic growth into the traditional sectors of the economy. While the advanced sector of industry was in crisis, faced with highly unionised workforces, which threatened the ability of firms to respond effectively to market conditions, small non-unionised firms thrived. It is these firms that have provided much of the vigour of the Italian economy in recent years, sometimes working as sub-contractors to the advanced sector, and sometimes producing directly for the consumer markets. The rapid economic growth in the North-Eastern regions of Emilia-Romagna, Friuli-Venezia-Giulia, and the Veneto owes much to this sector.[27] Recent figures show that in the decade 1971-81, the average size of units of production in industry has diminished sharply in all regions except in the South.[28] The growth of small-scale firms of the type described has also created certain problems for the government, in so far as they present problems of fiscal control; tax evasion and tax avoidance is a major issue facing the government.

Economic growth after 1983 saw a revitalisation of the Italian economy. The expansion of the world economy opened up export markets for Italian goods. The high value of the US dollar made Italian goods particularly competitive in important export markets. Meanwhile, at home, many of the major industrial firms finally put their house in order. Apart from the export opportunities, they were also helped by the declining strength of the union movement as a result of rising unemployment. The 1980 strike at Fiat marked an important turning point in relations between management and unions. The management held out on union demands. After more than a month, workers dissenting from the union line staged a right-to-work march through the streets of Turin. The strike collapsed. Management was back in control.

The next major step forward, as far as management was concerned, was the reform of the *scala mobile*. A minor reform was achieved by the Fanfani government in 1983. But it was only with the acession of the Craxi government that a major reform was finally achieved in 1984. The reform, reducing automatic wage increases below the rate of inflation, was fiercely contested by the Communist Party and their union allies. In June 1984, the government was forced into a referendum. They held firm and won the vote. Large-scale industry, most affected by the *scala mobile*, had removed an important barrier to its playing a dynamic role in the development of the Italian economy.

In the public sector, important changes also took place. Professor Romano Prodi was appointed to the presidency of IRI (the state holding company for large tracts of Italian industry), and set about the revitalisation of the state sector. Loss-making industries have been sold off, not to the public in the manner of British privatisations, but to private firms. Thus Alfa Romeo was sold to Fiat in late 1986. Those firms not sold off have been bullied into becoming more profitable. New managers have been appointed, no longer many of the incompetent political appointees of the past, but successful professional managers, often drawn from the private sector.

3. POLITICAL TRANSFORMATION

Turning to the post-war political transformation, the first point to emphasise with regard to the political system is the different bases of political relationships in North and South. The South resembles a clientelistic system, while the North is an associative system. Clientelism has changed substantially in the South over the past forty years. In the past, politics was dominated by local notables, who had only tenuous links with organised political parties. The relationship between elector and elected was direct and immediate. Favours were exchanged on a one-to-one basis.[29]

The organised political parties soon moved in to adapt the clientelistic system to their own needs. The local notables were either integrated into the political parties, or replaced by party managers. With direct access to State resources through their control of the central government, the party managers of the governing parties were able to develop a system of mass clientelism.[30] As the South has been particularly dependent on State resources compared to the North, the clientelistic system was an efficient mechanism for gaining political support. All parties active in the South have to some extent worked through the clientelistic system. As the dominant party of government, however, the Christian Democrats, have gained most advantage from the system. Economic problems during the 1970s and 1980s, which have limited the availability of State resources, are now limiting the effectiveness of clientelism.

While the South has few historical traditions of political ideology, the story is very different in Northern and Central Italy. The two major ideological traditions or 'families' are Catholicism and Socialism. During the early years of national unity, prior to the First World War, a third 'bourgeois' tradition was dominant. During this period, the franchise was extremely limited, and the political system was based on the concept of *trasformismo*. Local notables, loosely associated with the pro-system and bourgeois Liberal Party, sat in parliament, forming cabinets on the basis of shifting individual alliances. Though opposition groups developed, they were all pro-system. The Socialist Party developed with the extension of the franchise in the late nineteenth century. Drawing its support from the emerging working class in the North and rural areas in Central Italy, it was the first anti-system party. These regions, particularly Tuscany and Emilia-Romagna, are still major areas of Communist and Socialist strength in the 1980s. As for Catholicism, it too failed to emerge as a popular political force until the late nineteenth century. Apart from the question of the limited franchise, the nature of unification, involving the military defeat of the Vatican armies by Piedmont, had led the Pope to ban

Catholic participation in the institutions of the new state. This self-imposed exile of the Pope formally lasted till the signing of the Lateran Pacts with Mussolini in 1929. However, the growing appeal of Socialism to the masses had encouraged Catholics to enter the political fray so as not to allow the Socialists to win by default. This period saw the development of the Popular Party, led by the Sicilian priest Don Luigi Sturzo. Drawing its support largely from rural small-holders, particularly in North-Eastern Italy, the Popular Party was strongly orientated to social Catholicism, and did not always sit easily with Vatican conservatism. Like the Socialist Party, it was viewed by the political establishment as an anti-system party.[31]

The elections of 1919, following the introduction of universal male suffrage, revealed the strength of the anti-system parties. The Socialist and Popular parties won a majority of parliamentary seats. Their inability to form an alliance, and the fears of the bourgeois elite, contributed to the success of the Fascists in consolidating political power on a very slim electoral base. Fascism interrupted the development of the party system (from 1926, all rival political parties were banned), it also destroyed the credibility of the old bourgeois parties. The present day Liberal and Republican parties, heirs to the bourgeois tradition, enjoy only limited popular support. The Catholic and Socialist traditions, however, derived certain strengths from Fascism. The Lateran Pacts gave the Church a privileged cultural position within the State. Only in 1984 did a new Concordat come before parliament. When the Christian Democratic Party was formed, following the fall of Fascism, it was able to draw on the organisational strength of the Church. It drew also on the various legacies of Catholicism including that of the old Popular Party. It was, however, far broader in its social base than the old Popular Party. It became a truly interclassist party, aggregating elements of all social classes, including the bourgeoisie which had turned to the Christian Democrats as the best hope of defending their interests against Socialism.

The Socialists had entered the Fascist era as a divided movement. The maximalists had split from the party in 1921 to form the Communist Party. Both Communists and Socialists drew strength under Fascism from their organisational structure, which allowed them to play a prominent clandestine role, leading the Resistance Movement (there was no Resistance Movement in the South). At the end of the Second World War, the Communists and Socialists, ideologically close once again, were able to present a formidable pole of attraction on the Left.

The political history of the post-war era is concerned mainly with the process of accommodation (or lack of accommodation) between Socialism and Catholicism. Following the collapse of the early tripartite government

(Christian Democrats, Socialists, and Communists) in 1947, the Christian Democrats moved into coalition with the old bourgeois parties. In the Cold War atmosphere which pervaded the 1948 elections, the Christian Democrats scored a resounding victory. Despite having a majority of parliamentary seats, they governed in coalition with the Liberals, Republicans, and Social Democrats. The latter had split from the Socialist Party in 1948 in response to the pro-Communist stance of the Socialist Party. The Socialists and Communists, in fact, fought the 1948 elections on a joint list. The early defection of the Social Democrats to the government camp can be considered the first stage of accommodation between Socialism and Catholicism.

The next stage of accommodation occurred fifteen years later, in 1963, with the 'opening to the Left' proposed by Moro's Christian Democrats. Since 1948, the Socialists had remained in political isolation with the Communists. As Cold War tensions diminished, the Socialists, under Nenni's guidance, moved steadily towards the Centre. By 1963, they were ready to accept the offer of the Christian Democrats. The latter, for their part, had moved leftwards in response to the social upheavals that were taking place in the country. They felt the need to broaden their consensual base within the working class in order to ensure political stability. The Socialists saw the opportunity to push forward certain social reforms and institute greater State planning. They also saw the advantages of gaining access to the system of State patronage. The move of the Socialists to the Centre was cemented in their 1965 reunion with the Social Democrats.

By the end of the 1960s, the party strategies had gone badly wrong. The growing social unrest, culminating in the 'hot autumn', was evidence of failure. So, too, was the loss of electoral support of the new Unified Socialist Party at the 1968 elections. The Socialists had certainly gained benefits from sharing in the patronage system. Indeed, they had built up a clientelistic base in parts of the country. But, unable to bring a positive reforming image to the government, they lost much of their traditional support. The experiments with planning, copied from the French, had been unsuccessful. When social protest boiled over, the governing parties, and particularly the Socialists and Christian Democrats, moved sharply leftwards, trying to leave as little space as possible for the Communists as the voice of opposition. In the event, even this strategy was a failure. The government had underestimated the strength of the right-wing backlash which manifested itself in the 1972 elections. The neo-Fascist Italian Social Movement (MSI) made spectacular gains. In parts of the urban South, such as Catania, the neo-Fascists became the largest party. Overall, they gained 8.7 per cent of the vote, rivalling the Socialists for the position of Italy's third largest party.[32]

Partly as a result of the 1972 elections, the major parties (excluding the MSI) changed ideological direction. Subsequent years saw a narrowing of ideological differences. At the same time, party divisions increased in the sense that parties strove even harder to distinguish themselves from one another in the eyes of the electorate. The change in ideological direction occurred most dramatically in the Communist Party. Enrico Berlinguer, the party leader, proposed a 'historic compro-mise', which was, in effect, a government of national unity, linking all democratic parties in combatting Italy's social, economic, and civil crises. The Left, alone, Berlinguer felt, could not affront these crises. The experience of Chile showed the hazards of a narrowly-based, left-wing coalition coming to power. In addition, growing terrorism, particularly of the Right, which had begun in 1969 with the bombing of a Milanese bank in which fourteen people were killed, gave rise to fears of a neo-Fascist revival. The MSI electoral success of 1972 confirmed these fears. Finally, the demand for a 'compromise' was an admission that Catholicism existed in Italy as a potent political force, appealing to large sections of the working class.

As a political strategy, the 'historic compromise' was a resounding success in the short-run. Communists made substantial gains in the 1975 administrative elections, and in the 1976 legislative elections, they increased their share of the vote from 27.2 per cent to 34.4 per cent. They were now almost equal rivals with the Christian Democrats whose share of the vote slipped marginally from 39.1 per cent to 38.8 per cent. The smaller parties of the Centre, including the Socialists, were effectively squeezed out by the massive presence of Communists and Christian Democrats. After 1972, the Socialists were wary of continuing their participation in the government coalition, which had brought them so little electoral success. They withdrew in 1974, precipitating a crisis within the political system. Without the Socialists, the Christian Democrats found it difficult to form a stable coalition, unless they turned to either the Communists or the neo-Fascists. Neither of these options was attractive or even politically feasible. However, after the Communist electoral successes of 1976, and with the continued reticence of the Socialists, the Christian Democrats were obliged to make overtures to the Communists. By progressive stages, the Communists assumed a greater role in the governing majority, abstaining from voting against the government from 1976 to 1978, and giving it external support from 1978 to 1979. They never, however, obtained ministerial positions.

With only part of their strategy fulfilled, the Communists now found themselves in a dilemma. On the one hand, their support of a government which was now actively pursuing austerity measures alienated their traditional supporters in the northern working class. They were increasingly seen as part of the political establishment. (Significantly, political terrorism reached its peak during this period with the assassination of the Christian Democratic politician, Aldo Moro.) On the other hand, the Communists were unable to exercise effective control over the government. Reforms which bore their imprint, such as the *equo canone*, the fair rent law, were not successful. Indeed, this reform dried up the private rental market in Italy, affecting job and residential mobility. Thus, in 1979, the Communists withdrew their support of the government, provoking new elections. Their share of the vote declined sharply to 30.4%, while that of the Christian Democrats and the Centre parties held steady. The main beneficiary of the Communist Party's decline was the small anti-establishment Radical Party, which increased its share of the vote from 1.1% to 3.4%.

The withdrawal of the Communists was not as catastrophic for political stability as might have been thought a couple of years earlier. A brief resurgence of economic growth, though coupled with high inflation, had increased public contentedness. More important, the Socialist Party, under the dynamic leadership of Bettino Craxi, was once again ready to participate in a Centre coalition, either with or without the Communists. The price of Socialist participation was that there should be a measure a cabinet equality between the Christian Democrats and the parties of the lay Centre, of which the Socialists were one. The Socialists also argued that the premiership should not necessarily be held by a Christian Democrat. In the event, the Socialists accepted for the time being the premiership of the Christian Democrat, Cossiga, and later, of Forlani. When, in 1981, however, the P-2 corruption scandal weakened the moral authority of the Christian Democrats, the smaller parties were finally successful in having the premiership assigned to one of their own politicians. Craxi had been a candidate, but, politically, Spadolini, leader of the small Republican Party, was a more acceptable figure.

Spadolini's two administrations lasted till late 1982, when the Socialists withdrew their support. The Christian Democrats, in the meantime, had elected a new secretary, De Mita, to clean up their image. They were now ready to resume the premiership in the person of Fanfani, an elder statesman of the party. His government lasted just a few months, till once again the Socialists withdrew their support, and early elections were called.

The Socialists had hoped to make substantial gains in the elections. Public opinion polls had suggested they might double their vote, but such polls are notoriously unreliable in Italy (they always underestimate Communist support, for instance, and overestimate Socialist support).

The Socialists increased their vote by a modest 1.6% to 11.4%. The other small Centre parties backed this up with an increase of 3.4% to 12.1%. Now the lay Centre parties could claim to represent 23.1% of the electorate, a respectable third force in Italian politics between Christian Democrats and Communists. For the Christian Democrats, the elections were a disaster; their share of the vote plummetted to 32.8%; since 1948, it had never fallen below 38%. The Communist vote, meanwhile, held fairly steady at around 30%.

With their new image in disarray, the Christian Democrats were prepared to accept Craxi's leadership, but it was now their turn to exact a price. First, the Socialists had to modify their economic programme by agreeing to cut public expenditure and put a brake on labour costs (a price also exacted for Republican support); second, they had to make a firm commitment to the installation of Cruise missiles. Other less explicit commitments included Socialist acceptance of Christian Democratic superiority in the cabinet; the Christian Democrats were to have a cabinet majority, and the choice of ministers was to be made by the party leadership. Further, the Christian Democrats made it clear that they expected the Socialists to be willing to form coalitions at the level of local government. Following the Communist local election victories of 1975, the Socialists had formed left-wing coalitions with the Communists in many major cities. The Christian Democrats felt they had been excluded too long. By exacting these various commitments, the Christian Democrats hoped to create a stable and long-lasting alternative of the Centre, isolating the Communist Party, and denying the Socialists a chance of playing a pivotal role between Left and Centre. What the Christian Democrats had not reckoned upon was that Craxi would prove so hard to displace. The 1987 elections are a test of the relations of strength between two parties in any future coalition of the Centre.

In a sense, the problem of accommodation between Catholicism and Socialism is still not resolved. The Socialists may have enjoyed the luxury of playing a pivotal role between Christian Democracy and Communism, but they are not strictly representative of the working class. The political representatives of the working class, the Communist Party, remain excluded from the national political system and such exclusion creates an inherent instability in the political system, given the economic policy problems that governments of the 1980s are facing. The difficult relations between Socialists and Christian Democrats may yet allow the Communists to play a greater role after the 1987 elections. Talk of a compromise between Christian Democrats and Communists has been raised, though vigorously denied by both sides. A compromise would have the advantage for the Christian Democrats of regaining the premiership and dominating a stable coalition government, something which the Socialists have not allowed them to do for the past several years. For the Communists, it would give them entree to government.

4. CONCLUSION: MANAGING THE ECONOMY IN THE 1980s

The political and economic problems are closely linked in Italy. The economic success of the past few years had led many Italians to believe that government is irrelevant to economic growth. They may well be partially right about the recent past, where external factors played their part. But they are bound to look towards government again when expansion ends, as it is predicted to do in the near future.

Inflation is no longer a problem, but unemployment is increasing steadily, and as growth declines is likely to increase. The under-development of the South, which has not shared in northern prosperity remains to be tackled, and like unemployment will worsen in a recession. Meanwhile, throughout the 1980s, the public sector deficit has remained at worryingly high levels. All these problems will have to be tackled by government.

Let us take the example of the public sector deficit. The estimated deficit for 1987 is over Lit. 100,000,000, around 12% of gross national product. A public deficit of this size swallows up private investment capital, and predetermines monetary policy by pushing up interest rates. In addition, the sheer inefficiency of the public sector weighs heavily upon more vigorous sectors of the economy that in the end have to pay for it. The Craxi government produced a package of saving to deal with the public sector deficit. But these savings hardly made a dent. When economic growth came, Craxi felt safe in ignoring the deficit. Lower unemployment would lower state benefits payments and hence reduce the deficit. Growth would also lower the deficit as a proportion of gross national product. To some extent, Craxi's strategy was borne out. But as growth looks set to slow, the new government will have to tackle the deficit as one of the its priorities. Essentially, it has the option of cutting public expenditure or raising taxes.

The basic difficulty of raising revenue through taxation is that those who would pay are already highly taxed. Though Italy has a relatively low tax base, the average wage earner pays 40–50% of his earnings in taxes and social contributions. The large numbers of self-employed are adept at evading and avoiding taxes. Some reforms have been made in previous years to gather more taxes from the self-employed, and further reforms have been promised, but such reforms will clearly not be popular with the self-employed who constitute many of the government's supporters. Another illustration of the government's predicament over taxation concerns Treasury bills. Interest on these bills was only recently taxed, despite strong union pressure. However, simply taxing the bills would make them very difficult to sell, and given the size of the public deficit, it could result in the bankruptcy of the State. The solution chosen by the government was to levy a small tax at source, not declarable in income tax returns, and to raise the interest rates paid by the amount of the tax.

Cutting public expenditure is no simpler. A few cuts were made by the Craxi government in social security payments, further cuts may have to be made, particularly in the nationalised industries, where the government is only just beginning to tackle the problems of inefficiency and overcapacity. These cuts will increase unemployment (already over two million), and risk alienating the working class still further. These prospects worry all the parties, especially those with working-class support. In addition, parties are worried that in a system rife with political patronage, any spending cuts involve high political risk.

The harsh economic medicine that the government is trying to hand out is filled with pitfalls. So long as the working class remains politically excluded from the decision-making process, such policies could give rise to social unrest. Already in 1987 we are seeing a high level of work-place conflicts, not so much organised by the traditional unions, but by many of the autonomous unions that are particularly active in the public sector. The 1987 election, for instance, has taken place with intermittent black-outs of public service news coverage, as a result of autonomous strike action.

NOTES

1 Cf. A. King, ed., *Why is Britain Becoming Harder to Govern?*, BBC Publications, London, 1976.
2 Cf. S. N. Eisenstadt and R. Lemarchand, eds. *Political Clientelism, Patronage and Development*, Sage, London, 1981.
3 Cf. K. Allen and M.C. MacLellan, *Regional Problems and Policies in Italy and France*, Allen & Unwin, London, 1970.
4 Cf. A. Maddison, *Economic Growth in the West*, Twentieth Century Fund, New York, 1964, p. 28.
5 Cf. M. D'Antonio, *Sviluppo e Crisi del Capitalismo Italiano*, De Donato, Bari, 1973, op. 69, pp. 72, 59.
6 Cf. A. Maddison, op. cit., p. 28.
7 Cf. D'Antonio, op. cit., pp. 54–55.
8 Cf. *La Reppublica*, 6 March 1987.
9 *Ibid.*
10 Cf. *Financial Times*, 23 April 1987.

11 *Ibid.*
12 Cf. A. Maddison, op. cit.
13 C. Kindleberger, *Europe's Post-War Growth*, MIT Press, Cambridge, Mass., 1967.
14 ISTAT, *L'Italia*, Roma, 1983, p. 33.
15 Ibid., pp. 34, 71.
16 G.H. Hildebrand, *Growth and Structure in the Economy of Modern Italy*, Harvard University Press, Cambridge Mass., p. 69.
17 ISTAT, 1983, op. cit., p. 93.
18 Adapted from ISTAT, *Annuario Statistico Italiano*, Roma, 1982, p. 256.
19 Ibid., p. 250.
20 Cf. K. Allen and MacLellan, op. cit.; also S. Ronzani, 'Regional incentives in Italy', D. Yuill, K. Allen, and C. Hull, eds., *Regional Policy in the European Community*, Croom Helm, London, 1980.
21 S. Ronzani, op. cit., p. 135.
22 G. Mottura, and E. Pugliese, 'Mercato del lavoro e caratteristiche dell'emigrazione italiana nell'ultimo quindicennio', in P. Leon and M. Maroceni, eds., *Sviluppo Economico Italiano e Forza-Lavoro*, Marsilio, Padova, 1973, pp. 231-256.
23 Cf. Giunta Regionale Lombarda, Assessorato al Lavoro e Movimenti Demografici, *Conferenza Regionale sui Movimenti Demografici*, Villa Ponti, Varese.
24 For two contrasting views, cf. W.R. Bohning, 'Some thoughts on emigration from the Mediterranean Basin', in *International Labour Review*, Vol III, No 3, 1974, pp. 251-277; and K. Griffin, 'On the emigration of the peasantry', in *World Development*, Vol. 4, No 5, 1976, pp. 353-361.
25 V. Lutz, *Italy: a Study in Economic Development*, Oxford University Press, London, 1962.
26 Cf. G. Bianchi, R. Aglieta, P. Merli-Brandini, *I Delegati Operai: Ricerca su Nuove Forme di Rappresentanze Operaie*, Quaderni ISRIL, Roma, 1970.
27 On the Italian productive structure, cf. G. Fuà, *Occupazione e Capacità Produttiva: la Realtà Italiana*, Il Mulino, Bologna, 1976.
28 Cf. ISTAT 1983, op. cit., p. 52.
29 Cf. L. Graziano, 'Patron-client relationships in Southern Italy', in *European Journal of Political Research*, 1 April 1973, pp. 3-34.
30 J. Chubb, 'The social basis of an urban political machine: the Christian Democratic Party in Palermo', in S. N. Eisenstadt and R. Lemarchand, op. cit.; also M. Cacagli and F. P. Belloni 'the New Clientelism in Southern Italy: the Christian Democratic Party in Catania', Ibid.
31 On the Italian political system, cf. P. Allum, *Italy—Republic without Government?*, Weidenfeld & Nicolson, London, 1973; also S. H. Barnes, *Representation in Italy*, Chicago University Press, Chicago, 1977.
32 On parties' ideological changes, cf. A. Mastropaolo and M. Slater, 'Party platforms and electoral programmes in Republican Italy: 1946-1979', in I. Budge, D. Robertson, and D. Hearl, eds., *Ideology, Strategy and Party Movement: Spatial Analyses of Post-War Election Programmes in 18 Democracies*, Cambridge University Press, Cambridge, 1985.

THE POLITICS OF THE STATE STEEL INDUSTRY IN ITALY
THE ART OF MUDDLING THROUGH

John Eisenhammer

INTRODUCTION

CRISIS is a most common word in contemporary Italy. To believe newspaper opinion, party political rhetoric, managerial criticism, trade union protest, and much of academic evaluation, is to accept that the Italian economy is relentlessly pursuing a path towards collapse, and society towards division and conflict. Italy, by most accounts, languishes in a permanent crisis. But therein lies the contradiction, for few nations have done so much to devalue the word. Behind the rhetoric lies the more complex reality of a country that two decades ago enjoyed prodigious growth, and has since then continued to consolidate its strength and position as a major economic and industrial power. The prolonged recession has exacted a harsh toll on Italy, just as it has on other countries, but it is arguable whether Italy has fared much worse than many of its major competitors.

In terms of the insights it offers into Italy's post-war economic performance, the steel industry is both revealing and instructive. From relative insignificance, Italy rose at an exhilarating rate to the status of a major steel producer. Tenth in the world in 1953, Italy was sixth by 1979, and fourth after Japan, the United States and West Germany by 1982. Within Europe it rose from sixth to second place in the hierarchy of national producers during the same period. By 1983, Finsider, the Italian public sector steel holding, had become the second largest single producer in the world, after Nippon steel. This is by any account an extraordinary tale. Not least because, while the industry grew briskly during the boom years of the Fifties and Sixties, it achieved its present position by continuing to expand while rival steel industries pared back production and capacity under the weight of the recession.

This fact alone should inspire caution against too ready an acceptance of the simplistic rhetoric of the omni-present crisis. Like the elusive 'Republic without government', which nonetheless goes from strength to strength, is the steel sector an industry without management, which continues to survive, indeed to develop? Such evocative phrases reflect the persistent difficulty in achieving some general understanding of the way things function in Italian industry, economy and society. The oft-used phrase 'muddling through' merely acknowledges the fact that things are rarely what they seem. In a country where the institutional framework only approximates to the real configuration of power, where formal mechanisms are too often merely a front for very different procedures, where authority is diffused and accountability confused, how things 'really work' is sometimes quite simple, but almost always obscure. The fact remains, however, that despite all the apparent pitfalls and obstacles, the Republic, the economy, and particular industries, somehow manage to pull through.

How this has occurred in the case of the public sector steel industry in Italy is the subject of this study. A detailed analysis of the industry's post-war evolution is not attempted here, for it is not the central concern of the enquiry.[1] Rather, the broad characteristics of developments in the industry during the last thirty years are drawn upon insofar as they demonstrate some aspects of decision-making in Italy, and the nature of the political process in its relations with State-run industry.

THE SCOPE OF THE STUDY

This analysis is restricted to public sector steel in Italy, and moreoever, to bulk heavy steel making. This separation between public and private is not merely an intellectual device, but in fact follows existing divisions in production. Overall the public sector accounts for about 60 per cent of crude steel production, and 86 per cent of all flat products from its large integrated steel works at Taranto, Bagnoli, and Cornigliano.[2] The other major steel works at Piombino concentrates on long products. The high operating costs, and the continuous demand for high technology investment, has meant that only the State can afford to run these large scale integrated works. By contrast, 85 per cent of Italy's long products come from the private sector, where small producers using scrap-fuelled electric furnaces predominate.

At the top of the public sector steel hierarchy is the Institute for Industrial Reconstruction (IRI), initially set up by Mussolini in 1933 to supplement the supply of credit for the reorganisation of industry in Italy. In 1936 its powers were redefined to enable it to administer State participations; on the eve of the Second World War IRI controlled 45 per cent of net steel production. Over the years IRI has accumulated a steady stream of ailing industries; turning it into a vast umbrella organisation. Steel, however, remains one of its most important activities. IRI acts as the link between the government, and in particular the Minister for State Participations, and the industrial sector itself. It is a channel for funds, an overall coordinator, and a crucial agent in the elaboration of industrial strategy.

The parent company of public sector steel is Finsider, an IRI subsidiary. It was formed in 1937 to take responsibility for the technical coordination of iron and steel making. In the beginning IRI only possessed a little over 50 per cent of the shares in Finsider—the so-called IRI formula of financing which aroused such international interest in the Fifties—but the recession has obliged the State progressively to assume full control. The most important of Finsider's subsidiaries is Italsider, founded in the Sixties. Running eight works in all, employing some 53,000 people in 1980, its production is concentrated in the already mentioned integrated coastal steel complexes at Taranto, Cornigliano, Bagnoli and Piombino, which account for nearly all of Italy's pig iron production, and just under half of its steel.

THE YEARS OF EXPANSION

It has only been in the last few years that the full rigours of the world recession have come to bear upon the Italian steel industry, revealing most clearly that its difficulties are not dissimilar from those of its struggling rivals. During the Seventies, and even into the Eighties, steel making in Italy presented something of an enigma, mainly because it stood out in such marked contrast to what was happening to similar sectors in other parts of the industralised world. In the European Economic Community (EEC) some 260,000 steel workers lost their jobs between 1974 and 1982 (in addition to 130,000 in the USA). Steel making capacity was substantially reduced, as consumption weakened and prices tumbled. The brutal contraction of the steel industry exposed, in a most dramatic manner, the decline of traditional sectors and often the dilapidation of entire regions. But what the general statistics obscure is that while steel making capacity north of the Alps was being cut back in great swathes, in Italy it was actually increasing. Employment rose from 94,000 in 1974 to 101,000 by 1980, while productive capacity grew from 29 million tonnes in 1974, to a claimed 41 million tonnes in 1981.

A combination of three factors is needed to explain how such a situation was possible: Italy's productivist managerial culture, trade union power, and a tradition of State assistance. Firstly, steel making in Italy represents, or at least represented until only very recently, something qualitatively different in the minds of its industrialists,

politicians and unionists from what it does among its northern
competitors. In France, Britain and Germany, all nations with long
industrial traditions where whole communities have lived for generations
to the rhythm of the forge and furnace, the steel industry of today stands
more as testament to the past than as a promise for the future. The very
terminology of traditional, or 'smokestack' industry carries with it the
notion of decline, a process that can be slowed, but not arrested.

In Italy by contrast, the giant steel complexes stand as a powerful
statement of the country's only recently acquired industrial strength and
prowess. For Italy is a youth among the great industrial societies. Even
on the eve of the Second World War, with the nation ruled by a dictator
whose vision was based largely on might, total steel production was only
1.6 million tonnes in 1937 (the year that saw the foundation of
Finsider). In 1945 the task facing the nation was not so much
reconstruction as construction. A large steel industry was not only to
provide the foundations for growth; it was simultaneously to fuel and to
feed off that growth.

Thus only in the early 1950s did Italy enter the era of mass steel
making as Oscar Sinigaglia, the first Chairman of Finsider, carried out
his plan to provide the country with a modern steel industry,
concentrated mainly in advanced integrated steel complex situated on the
coast. Sinigaglia's programme was not only avant-garde in terms of steel
making, but above all represented an entirely new mentality: it sought to
transform Italy into a great industrial nation. Sinigaglia renovated the
older works at Bagnoli (Naples) and Piombino, which were to provide
the heavy materials for construction. But the clearest sign of Sinigaglia's
design came from Cornigliano (Genova). Production there concentrated
on plates and sheets, needed for the automobiles, the electrical goods, the
whole range of consumer durables which were to be both the motor and
the symbol of Italy's industrial awakening.[3] Between 1958 and 1963
automobile production in Italy tripled. Per capita steel consumption
soared from 50 kilogrammes in 1950 to 378 kilogrammes in 1970.

This expansionist surge forged a productivist managerial culture in
Italy which saw the steel industry not, as in many of its northern
partners, as a potential drain on industrial change, but as representing
the very thrust of that change. As the recession grew more menacing
during the late Seventies, the almost unanimous response of those
concerned with the future of steel making in Italy was to expand, to
modernise plant, to lead the way out of economic crisis.

The second factor to understand concerns the trade unions and labour
relations. Much has already been written on the effects of dislocation, of
the transition from a predominantly rural to a factory environment. The

accumulation of these tensions and contradictions exploded in the 'hot autumn' of 1969. The shockwaves unleashed by this dramatic series of events continued to perturb the industrial relations system right up until the early Eighties. At the risk of oversimplification, it can be said that organised labour in Italy came of age. From weak, divided organisations with little shop floor strength and only limited legitimacy, Italian unions were transformed by a vigorous unitary push from below into a powerful force. Within the space of a few years, the unionised worker in Italy became one of the best protected in Europe. The Federazione Lavoratori Metalmeccanici (FLM), formed in 1972 after a period of experimental unitary action between the three metalworkers federations (CGIL–FIOM, CSIL–FIM, UIL–UILM), played a key role in this process of transformation of Italian unionism. It became the symbol of labour's new found strength and confidence. From the shop floor to the national level the unions, often in alliance with the Communists (PCI) and other left-wing parties, used their greatly increased leverage not just to obtain generous wage increases, but also in attempts to influence decisions on a much broader range of issues, such as investment and work practices.

The consequences of accommodating a work force which, especially in the public sector, had acquired a position of some strength vis-à-vis management, could be relatively easily absorbed during a time of growth. But as the recession tightened, so the rigidity of labour practices, and the protection of vested interests, began rapidly to erode competitiveness. The burden of the huge fixed costs characteristic of the large scale integrated steel complexes was compounded by the seemingly inexorable rise of wage costs which far outstripped those of Italy's major European rivals.[4] Conflict became almost endemic, giving Italy the worst industrial relations record in European steel. Between 1969 and 1978, eight million tonnes of steel production were lost by Finsider due to strikes.[5] For the unions, the route of the steel industry in the face of the growing economic difficulties was forward—to modernise and to expand, especially in the more depressed regions of the country. Above all, jobs had to be safeguarded at all cost and, if possible, new ones created. Even when industrial and economic considerations may have dictated otherwise, the imperatives of maintaining social peace meant that union demands had, if not to be met in their entirety, at least to be compromised upon. As the difficulties afflicting public sector steel became more manifest, employers still found it impossible to challenge the basic assumption that employment levels had to be maintained. This partly explains the increasing use of *cassa integrazione guadagni* (the State assisted temporary lay-off scheme) from the late Seventies onwards, as a means of reducing labour costs for individual firms rather than attempting to push through formal redundancies. But this unwillingness to reduce employment levels, even in instances of patent over-manning, also reflected the pervasive influence of the tradition whereby the State provided funds and job opportunities. Quite simply, redundancies were not, until very recently, part of Italy's industrial vocabulary—social harmony and political stability had to be bought, regardless of cost.

The third factor, which is linked to the second, is the impact on public sector steel of growing governmental concern about the 'Southern question'. While the negative effects of the economic miracle found expression in the dormitory suburbs of the northern industrial centres, they were devastatingly evident in the impoverished South. Inequality between the two Italies was in fact widening, as the Mezzogiorno was left behind, progressively emptied of its most productive inhabitants. In an attempt to correct the growing regional imbalance, the government strove to push funds, employment and wealth into those backward areas. As a result, industrial and economic imperatives had to vie with social and political concerns in shaping the future of the steel industry. As the recession worsened, while the falling orders and rising losses may have forcefully stated the case for rationalisation and retrenchment, the whole weight of the government's southern policy and the tradition of assistance, pushed in favour of protecting jobs and plant, and even, if possible, of expansion.

The most striking result of the government's efforts towards the South was the giant steel complex at Taranto. Built in the Sixties, and later doubled in size to become the largest integrated steelworks in Europe, it represented the fusion of all three factors we have been discussing—the urge to achieve industrial greatness, the unions' determination to create jobs, and the urgency of the need to alleviate southern distress. Taranto graphically illustrates the phrase 'Cathedrals in the desert', for in addition to the steelworks, the entire industrial infrastructure had to be built virtually from scratch. Clearly the costs of such a policy were high, but they were deemed necessary in terms of social stability and national integration, not to mention the less public, but no less powerful interests of political patronage and clientilism.

The combination of these three elements transformed public sector steel making in Italy, certainly against the trend of more recent times, turning Italy into a giant among steel producing nations. But they were also instrumental in making it a giant with feet of clay. For while technically much of its plant is among the best in the world, its financial condition and capacity for adjustment are among the worst. For just as the rapid development of the steel industry since the Second World War epitomises that of Italy's political economy as a whole, so equally characteristic are the absence of any serious planning, the errors and misdeeds for which the taxpayer will eventually have to pay, and the delays and disruptions caused by bureaucratic inertia, social conflict and political division. Just as the three elements discussed above encouraged a growth-promotion response to the international steel crisis, so they tended to build that same expansion on a financial structure that was seriously flawed. Funding growth out of debts had been the preferred, if not necessary, manner of operating during the fat years of the economic miracle, and became to a degree ingrained in the Italian managerial psyche. For their part the trade unions, until late in the Seventies, showed little inclination to temper their bargaining strength with awareness of financial realities, and even when they did decide to do so, the national organisations had only marginal success in imposing restraint on the rank and file. And, lastly, when planning the future of steel, there were many among the decision makers who regarded uneconomically high costs as a necessary price to pay for social harmony, patronage and votes. It is to this duality—between industrial modernity and financial debility that we now turn. For an understanding how such a situation arose is richly revealing about how things really work in Italy, as well as an eloquent example about what, for want of a better term, has already been referred to as the 'art of muddling through'.

DEBTS AND POLITICS

The precarious state of public sector steel finances dates back to well before 1974. But the crucial difference, as has already been suggested, was that at that time debts were not held to be a problem. Indeed, deficit-financing was to a great extent the norm. In the heady days of the Fifties and Sixties demand was pulling ahead so briskly that industry was doing all it could just to keep pace. All effort was put into producing more and building more plant. The youthful steel industry did not have vast accumulated profits from the past to reinvest. So investment in the new forges, furnaces and mills, requiring massive capital outlays with long pay-back periods, meant that vast sums of money had to be borrowed. But the prospect of building virtually an entire industry on debt raised few eyebrows, for rates of interest were low, and so borrowing to increase production seemed a sensible way to operate.

Already by 1974 own resources represented a mere 14 per cent of Finsider's total capital investment, the rest being funded out of debt (including 32 per cent short term loans). By contrast ten other major European competitors had an average of 46 per cent of total investments covered by own resources, with a much smaller reliance on short term loans.[6] Similar figures apply to Italsider, which by 1976 already had debt servicing charges amounting to over 17 per cent of its turnover.[7]

But there was always the risk that while great efforts had been expended to modernise much of the steel industry, the advantages thus gained would be gravely threatened by the financial consequences of such modernisation. And indeed that is precisely what occurred. For when the recession hit, profits slumped and interest rates soared. Debts which at one time had fuelled the industry's expansion became a crushing burden, and a drain on State resources. The industrial performance of even potentially efficient plant became handicapped by a decrepit financial structure, under increasing strain because of a growing lack of funds.

One episode which spans precisely this transition from boom to recession concerns the proposal for building a fifth integrated steel complex. It underscores both the growth—orientated mentality and the fierce pressure from many quarters—industrial, political and labour—to modify their strategies in the light of rapidly changing economic conditions. The events surrounding the proposed fifth steel complex demonstrate the complex cross-pressures bearing upon the formulation and application of steel policy, and the extent to which industrial policy in Italy became politicised in the Seventies.

The confidence of Italy's steel producers in the late Sixties had expressed itself in the doubling of the Taranto works. With five blast furnaces and a potential capacity of 10.5 million tonnes it became the largest steel complex in Europe. In the early Seventies, as work on expanding Taranto went ahead, the government was forecasting an economic growth rate of six per cent per annum, with steel consumption rising to 25, 5 million tonnes nationally by 1975, and to 30 million tonnes by 1980. [8] Such expectations of prodigious growth persuaded the powers that be of the need for a fifth integrated steel works. While Finsider would have preferred to situate the new works nearer the markets, both European and domestic, in Northern Italy, the entire weight of government policy in favour of the Mezzogiorno was brought to bear. With attention therefore concentrated on the South, the problem became one of finding an area that had not already benefited in some way from government largesse. From the outset, economic and industrial considerations were relegated to secondary position, as social needs, regional policy, party influence, patronage and political ambitions vied for leverage over the decision-making process. Most importantly, this was also the moment when the trade unions decided to mobilise behind a renewed effort to influence investment and industrial strategy. The fifth steel centre was allocated by the CIPE (the Interministerial

Committee for Economic Planning) to Gioia Tauro—a sleepy Calabrian town—in response to increasing social discontent in the region. Already dissatisfied with the nature of decision-making involved, Finsider cautiously and quietly attempted to dissociate itself from the affair. It had already examined Gioia Tauro in the past and had found it unsuitable; not only would the entire infrastructure for a steel plant, including a port, have to be built from scratch but the zone was one of high seismic risk. [9] However, once decided upon the money, interests and prestige involved meant that the choice rapidly developed an internal dynamic which was hard to resist. While it was not long before most of those involved realised that the project was impracticable, it was many years before most of the proposals were discarded, and to this day it has still not been completely quashed.

The project originally aimed to build a steel complex capable of producing annually 4.5 million tonnes of flat laminates, providing 7,500 jobs. Since almost everything had to be built from scratch, vast sums of money were involved, which soon attracted the *'ndrangheta*, the Calabrian mafia. But even before the project left the drawing board, the energy crisis and its cumulative effects were already changing the outlook for the steel industry. The idea of building an entire integrated steel works was dropped by 1975, and over the following years the remaining plans for some form of steel making activity continued to be slimmed down. But while reducing the actual size and scope of the works, every effort continued to be made to ensure that jobs would still be created for the originally projected work force of 7,500. Similarly, lucrative contracts continued to be handed out for creating infrastructure, even though by the mid-Seventies the potential capacity of the works had been reduced to 1 million tonnes, far too small for the plant to be economically viable. Construction continued in belated fashion, despite the uncertainty and constant revisions, and indeed still went on after 1977–78 when the project had to all intents and purposes been scrapped.

Gioia Tauro lived on for two main reasons. Firstly the unions and a number of concerned politicians were determined not to see it die until something was found to replace it. Partly for this reason, and in spite of initial opposition from the IRI technical committee the 1979 steel plan deliberately budgeted for a cold rolling mill at Gioia Tauro. Giorgio Benvenuto, general secretary of the *Unione Italiana del Lavoro*, remarked,

A noi, interessa l'insediamento di Gioia Tauro. Finché non ci sono proposte alternative concrete e di pari occupazione, non si tocca. Non siamo così

ottusi da non sapere che c'è una crisi dell' acciaio. Però, non siamo
nemmeno così ingenui da accontarci di promesse vaghe.[10]

Beyond their concerns with employment, the unions were keen to
retain the project on the steel policy agenda for its symbolic value as a
bargaining counterpiece. Secondly, Gioia Tauro was kept alive as a
means of drawing in EEC funds. Donat Cattin, then Minister for
Industry, admitted that considerable sums were set aside for Gioia Tauro
in the 1979 steel plan, even though few people expected the investments
to be realised, as 'un elemento di scambio per ottenere adeguate
contropartite comunitarie per quanto concerne gli investimenti'.[11] By
1978 the scope of the proposed works had been reduced to a cold rolling
mill producing just 200,000 tonnes, but even this seemed destined to
remain on paper. To this day Gioia Tauro remains a sleepy Calabrian
town, except that down at the sea-front work goes on building the port
that has yet to find a convincing reason for its existence.

But Gioia Tauro did serve one useful purpose. For the Italians it
became their first major sacrifice in the face of the steel crisis. Though it
only ever existed on paper whenever the other European countries,
brandishing their massive capacity cuts, chasten the Italian government
for not doing its fair share, one of Finsider's first reactions is to proclaim
the example of Gioia Tauro, and of the sacrifice of the 4.5 million tonnes
that never were.[12]

CRISIS? WHAT CRISIS?

But the ignominious collapse of the plans for a fifth steel plant, while
suggesting growing tensions and inconsistencies within and between the
various groups responsible for steel policy, did not indicate anything
approaching a comprehensive reassessment of the steel industry's growth
plans in the light of the recession. In marked contrast to the prevailing
mood in the rest of the EEC, Finsider exuded a barely qualified air of
optimism, tinged with an element of defiance.

This rested on two central considerations. First, Italy remained a net
importer of steel products; during the mid-Seventies imports covered 30
per cent of domestic consumption. Notably, Italy was an importer of
large quantities of flat products, demand for which remained far more
dynamic than for longs. Of especial concern were coils, in which Italy
suffered a particular deficiency. About 40 per cent of home consumption
was covered by imports in the late Seventies, mostly from France and
Germany.

The second consideration was consumption. While fluctuating

considerably, the overall trend seemed to suggest that there was still room for increased consumption, and hence production.[13] Such a view was reinforced by the low rate of *per capita* steel consumption in Italy, compared with that of its major competitors. While there remained hope of consumption continuing to pull ahead, the dominant growth-orientated ethos lent towards an attacking strategy designed to capture the home market by massive import substitution, while mounting a determined export drive.

This required a shift in product mix towards coils, with an overall increase in the production of flat laminates. It is in this context that the major investments of the Seventies need to be seen—the completion of Taranto, the new forge and plant upgrading at Cornigliano; the proposed restructuring at Bagnoli. Overall, between 1974 and 1979 Italian steel making capacity rose from 29 million tonnes to 37 million tonnes. While the steel industry in the rest of Europe shed some 100,000 jobs between 1975 and 1979, employment in Italian steel rose by 2,000 to reach 98,000. The 1979 steel plan fully endorsed this optimistic outlook.

> La nostra struttura produttiva ... è fondamentalmente sana e competitiva; essa vuole misurarsi nei comparti più nobili, a più alto valore aggiunto, e non può accettare ipotesi di congelamento di crescita che impediscono di trarre giovamento da questa relativa 'giovinezza' degli impianti rispetto alla tradizione siderurgica degli altri partners europei.[14]

The plan posited very ambitious forecasts regarding growth in demand. This was expected to rise to between 23 and 24.8 million tonnes by 1981, and to between 27 and 30 million tonnes by 1985.[15] It was this claimed 'intensità dei consumi', as well as the relative modernity of much of Italian plant, that the government used in its argument to resist EEC demands for capacity cuts.

> La siderurgia italiana—a differenza di altre siderurgie europee—non dovrebbe attuare riduzioni complessive di capacità produttiva nell'arco dei prossimi anni, in funzione sopratutto della relativa 'modernità' degli impianti.[15]

Overall Finsider outlined investments worth 1,800 billion lire, over half of which were to be directed towards upgrading the Italsider plants at Cornigliano and Bagnoli.[17] Alongside Taranto, these two works were to be the driving force behind the attempt to overcome Italy's deficiency in flat laminates. The most important part of the strategy concerned the proposed restructuring of Bagnoli. This was one of the oldest steelworks in Italy, dating back to the beginning of the twentieth century. Its primary area had been modernised in the Sixties, but its downstream plant, the rolling mills, were antiquated and inefficient. Losing about 100 billion lire per annum in the late Seventies, Bagnoli placed a severe strain on Italsider's already hard pressed resources. Economically the plant ought to have been shut down. Certainly this was the considered view of the EEC Commission in Brussels. But Bagnoli, situated in languishing Naples, was a clear case where social considerations alone made such a course unthinkable for the Italian government. The politicians and the unions wanted jobs preserved, and Finsider wanted greater capacity for coils production. The combination of these two factors pushed the issues of economic viability, and of finding the necessary funds, into the background, as the decision to make Bagnoli a major centre for coils production was confirmed. In so doing the 1979 plan underscored the belated and incomplete nature of the Italian government's understanding of the steel crisis, despite the fact that by that time Finsider had accumulated debts of nearly eight thousand billion lire. The relevant decision-making bodies were nowhere near reaching that degree of awareness and general agreement that would have enabled them realistically to appraise the overall constraints of the recession, and to formulate an appropriate strategy for crisis management in steel. Not only were many of the industrialists and trade unionists still operating on the basis of a growth-focussed industrial culture that had long been superseded, but many politicians continued to act on considerations of patronage and social assistance which harked back to easier times. A ministerial committee deliberately increased the 1979 plan's consumption forecast—from the one advised by IRI—in order to justify the proposed work at Bagnoli and Gioia Tauro.[18] Such actions reflected less a mood of optimism than of irresponsibility, one marked by an inability or unwillingness to accept that Italy was in dire straits similar to those of its northern neighbours.

THE 1981 PLAN

This strategy of expansion, of maintaining the export drive while increasing Finsider's share of the home market, was confirmed in a White Paper produced by Assider in 1980. It stated that 'without any doubt' there was room for increased consumption of steel in Italy.[19] A similar line was expressed in the public sector steel plan approved by the Comitato dei Ministri per il Coordinamento della Politica Industriale (CIPI) in October 1981.[20] Circumstances, however, had changed not inconsiderably since 1979, explaining why the previous 1979 plan had had to be discarded and a new one hastily prepared. The recession, rather than abating, was deepening, and the steel crisis was assuming ever more worrying proportions. In Brussels a state of open crisis had already been declared with stricter national quotas, and in August 1981 the EEC introduced more rigorous controls on government aid to the steel industry. By 1981 employment had dropped 34 per cent since 1974 in the European Coal and Steel Community countries. In Italy, too, the statistics offered little cause for celebration. Although employment still held up—it increased by 6 per cent between 1974 and 1981—the figures did not reveal the true picture. The persistent inability to bring about redundancies—particularly in the public sector—was compensated for by the use of *cassa integrazione*, first introduced by Italsider in 1977 for 6,500 people. 1980, despite being a record year for consumption (25.6 million tonnes), saw *cassa integrazione* being resorted to for another 5,000 workers at Taranto and in Liguria, as Italsider ran up annual losses of nearly 750 billion lire (out of an accumulated debt of 4,500 billion lire). The manifest inability of Finsider to take advantage of the record consumption underlined its weakness. Imports flooded into the country, pushing the steel balance of payments back into the red for the first time since 1973. In a fit of desperation the Italian government closed several border posts to steel imports, but they were soon reopened on EEC orders. Italsider, with debt servicing charges that had reached a staggering 20 per cent of turnover by 1980, was facing a serious liquidity crisis. Towards the end of the year it was claiming that it could only pay its labour force and foreign suppliers. Pietro Sette, then President of IRI, warned 'Se non si procederà velocemente ad un' adeguata ricapitalizzazione della Finsider si dovrà giungere in breve tempo ad effettuare consistenti tagli nell' occupazione.'[21]

The 1981 CIPI plan did make some concessions to this unfavourable climate. It forecast more modest progress in steel consumption and projected reductions in the total labour force amounting to 8,000 jobs by 1985, to be achieved through natural wastage and early retirement.[22] Redundancies still remained anathema. However, the central thrust of previous steel policy of expansion and modernisation was confirmed. 'Nel loro insieme, i dati quantitativi esposti (nel piano) prospettano una sensibile espansione del ruolo della siderurgia Finsider, sia sul mercato interno che su quello internazionale'.[23]

But the persistence of such a commitment to growth showed little appreciation of the disastrous state of public finances. The 1981 plan assumed recapitalisation of Finsider for the period 1981–1983 amounting to 3,400 billion lire, as well as another 3,940 billion lire for investment.[24] But IRI, with a vast panoply of mostly loss-making commitments, was in no position to provide such funds. And central government itself was increasingly hard pressed. The social security system was absorbing vast sums of money. In short, a State geared to expansion and assistance was revealing itself to be structurally incapable of dealing with its catastrophic finances. With the recession deepening, currency instability growing, inflation high and interest rates mounting, getting the public sector deficit under control had become imperative. Recognition of this fact, and expressions of willingness to take the harsh measures required, began to be heard in some political quarters. For those concerned with introducing some degree of accountability and order into public finances the steel industry, the major cause of IRI's debts, was an obvious case for attention.

FUNDING PUBLIC SECTOR STEEL

In now turning to look more closely at the different attitudes within the government towards the funding of public sector steel, and just how such funding actually works as opposed to how it was meant to operate in theory, the discussion attempts to shed some light on the complex nature of decision-making and the political process in Italy. Italian governments are not known for their homogeneity. They are made up, not only of different parties, but also of a balance between the various factions in the major parties (mainly the Christian Democrats). Government coalitions, always a precarious political compromise, rarely survive for very long, making it difficult to establish a coherent line of activity. The notion of collective responsibility barely exists in any real sense, giving much of government activity an inconsistent and even contradictory nature. Two ministers can promise totally different things, or as will be seen below, one minister can commit the government to a certain action while another, whose cooperation is necessary, simply fails to deliver on such promises.

As the public sector deficit swelled to worrying proportions under the weight of the recession (over 15 per cent of GDP by 1982, a world record for an industrialised country) and Finsider's losses, contrary to the forecasts, continued to mount, there began in the early Eighties to emerge within the government two different approaches to the future of Italy's public sector steel industry. The then Socialist Minister for State Participations, Gianni De Michelis, exemplified those in favour of maintaining the State's commitment to the industry, and of continuing to advance Italy's cause on the world market. His approach was based largely on considerations of industrial strength and jobs—very much within the tradition of State assistance. On such a view, the State needed 'to have the courage to spend'; to increase its massive debts in an effort to modernise and to grow its way out of the crisis. This line was not shared by other, and ultimately more important, figures in the cabinet at the time. The Republican Budget Minister, Giorgio La Malfa, and the Christian Democrat Treasury Minister, Nino Andreatta, were constrained by their functions to pursue a strategy of strict public finances. They insisted that the government could no longer afford to hand out money unconditionally. As far as the public sector was concerned, no funds would be given unless they were backed up by comprehensive proposals designed to make the industry economically viable. If this meant cutbacks, then so be it.

Events in early 1981 dramatically illustrated the clash between these two positions. Finsider, facing one of its recurrent liquidity crises, insisted that it was on the brink of collapse, and that it could only afford to pay 70 per cent of its wage force. In response, De Michelis, on 26 February, announced aid worth over 5,000 billion lire for the public sector steel industry and ordered IRI immediately to find 30 billion lire to pay the full wage of Finsider's employees. Furthermore, De Michelis assured trade unionists that employment levels would be maintained in the State steel sector. The problem was that these moves did not have the backing of either La Malfa or Andreatta, who effectively controlled the purse strings. In fact in a letter to De Michelis and to Sette (President of IRI) the Treasury Minister emphasised that he would not lift a finger to pay out the sums of money promised by his colleague.[25]

Such inconsistencies seriously impeded the government's ability to exercise adequate control over affairs in the State steel sector. Above all, it was most unsettling for the steel producers themselves who had to operate in an atmosphere of sometimes baffling uncertainty. One direct consequence of this state of affairs was that IRI and Finsider not infrequently resorted to melodramatic threats of imminent collapse to jolt the government into action. We have just seen how in February 1981 Finsider claimed its inability to pay all of its wages in an effort to stir the government into providing it with urgently needed extra funds. Later, in another episode in September 1982, Finsider suddenly demanded *cassa integrazione* for an unprecedented 20,000 workers and claimed that it had orders for only one more month.

Management in Rome knew that such a request would never be accepted, but that was not the subject of the exercise. For what was really being sought were funds, to breathe life into Finsider's cash-starved plants, and it was well appreciated that there was nothing like the spectre of closures and widespread job losses, especially in the South, to spur the government into quickly releasing some cash. Carrying the burdensome legacy of undercapitalisation from its days of rapid debt-fuelled growth, Finsider's continued unwillingness or inability to cut back substantially on loss-making plant meant that its demand for capital injections from the government became ever more pressing. The persistent undercapitalisation of the public enterprises has had the consequence, deliberate or otherwise, of making them much more exposed to political control. Instead of disposing of regularly allocated funds with which they could subsequently act independently, the State sector firms are dependent on the continued bargaining of the political process as they strive to gain as much influence as possible in the allocation of resources.

It is in such a light that much of the rhetoric and histrionics which colour day to day politics in Italy needs to be seen. This effervescence on the surface reflects the constant and complex struggle for influence and a greater share of the State's overstretched resources in a system where funds are often allocated less on a structured basis than on the needs and imperatives of the moment.

The effects of these very different attitudes towards public sector funding within the government become more apparent when seen in terms of how such funding, in the case of steel, actually works. The nature and extent of State aid to industry in most countries, particularly when such aid is subject to restrictions (in this case the EEC) is never an easy matter to identify and to quantify. In Italy, a financial mechanism which is by its very nature perplexing in its ramifications and confusing in its procedure makes the task that much more difficult. So we must restrict ourselves here to a general appraisal of the problem. For our purpose, an analysis of Law 675 of 1977 on industrial reconstruction and reconversion is highly revealing about the differences between how the funding mechanism in Italy is supposed to operate, and how it in fact works.

Law 675 was designed to channel funds into key industrial sectors with a minimum of political fuss and bureaucratic delay. Its operation was very simple in theory. In the case of steel a Finsider works for example would make a case for State funds on the basis of a viable restructuring plan. This would be conveyed to a credit institution which would then evaluate the proposals. If approved, the credit institution handed the dossier on to the Ministerial Committee for the Coordination of Industrial Policy (CIPI), the implication being that by presenting it to the government the credit institution was in fact willing to participate in funding the proposed investments. If approved by the CIPI, the go-ahead was given for the credit institution to release the funds, which were guaranteed by the State. While the aided steelworks paid only 8 per cent on the loan, the credit institution received the market rate, the difference being made up by the government.

Unfortunately things never worked like this. Far from overcoming bureaucratic delay, the law became a monument to administrative imcompetence and political obfuscation. It became even more nefarious when combined with the lethargic intricacies of the banking system. As far as steel is concerned, though the law was instituted in 1977, it was not until early 1983 that the first petty sums trickled into Finsider's empty coffers. However, confusion in understanding what was really happening stemmed from the fact that on several occasions vast sums of money were committed on paper by government ministers to specific restructuring and development projects. The 1979 Plan allocated nearly 1,300 billion lire (including a large amount for Bagnoli) under Law 675 but it never arrived. Again in January 1981 the CIPI allocated 1,068 billion lire for similar projects but it, too, never materialised. In October 1982 the Industry Minister signed a decree ordering, yet again, the credit institutions to give out under Law 675 the funds for the restructuring of Bagnoli, but to no avail. In this way thousands of billion of lire were promised, and signed away with due pomp and ceremony. This led many people to believe that public sector steel had received vast amounts of money. Indeed, on at least two occasions, the funds allocated to be spent under Law 675 were reported to have been exhausted. For on paper the money had been allocated, often many times over for the very same investment, but in reality not a lira had changed hands. The major difficulty was one that has already been alluded to; while one minister could promise funds, another responsible for paying them out simply refused to do so. But the situation was rendered even more complex by the fact that even when the proposed funds apparently had the backing of the entire CIPI, they still failed to materialise.

This proved to be a disastrous situation for the credit institutions, for the State guarantee on their easy loans was no guarantee at all. Moreover, the credit institutions were being asked to evaluate requests for loans on the basis of national steel plans which, by the time it came to hand over the funds, had either been superseded by a revised plan, or had been rejected by the EEC. Since State aid to the steel industry requires prior EEC approval, this placed the banks and credit institutions in an invidious position.

But neither could Finsider just sit back and wait until government ministers agreed on what funding was both necessary and available. Major restructuring, already slipping behind schedule, had to be continued. In particular, Finsider was building an entire new hot strip mill at Bagnoli, with which it hoped to win a larger share of the still relatively dynamic coils market. This investment alone was estimated at some 1,000 billion lire. But if the State would not provide this money, it had to be found elsewhere—and that meant on the open market. While banks were unwilling to lend on the terms of Law 675, they were prepared to cover themselves by lending at full market rates. These were very high, over 20 per cent in the late Seventies, rising to 26 per cent in 1981. The banks were confident that even though Finsider was financially debilitated, the government would not permit public sector steel to collapse. To this extent at least, their loans were covered by the State. Similarly, Finsider's managers, though piling up colossal debts (in 1981 Finsider's accumulated debt equalled its turnover), and with no hope of ever paying them back, were prepared to continue this *fuite en avant* in the knowledge (or the hope) that one day the State would bail them out. By the early Eighties the percentage of indebtedness towards credit institutions of public enterprises generally, in comparison to their total sales, was about double that of the private sector, (44 per cent to 23 per cent respectively).

Public sector steel in Italy is built on a vast mountain of IOUs. In 1979 Finsider's total capital investment was covered by only nine per cent of its own resources.[26] The rest was funded from debt, including some 41 per cent of short term loans. By 1980 the situation was worse still, as Finsider's own resources made a mere five per cent of its capital investment. Only Nippon steel, with total investment covered to 19 per cent by its own resoures, came anywhere near matching Finsider's position. But the Japanese loans were on very favourable terms, so that debt servicing charges were under six per cent of turnover. By contrast, Finsider's desperation for funds, forcing it to contract loans at exorbitant rates, meant that it was carrying debt servicing charges amounting to a staggering 20 per cent of its turnover. The State sector steel in Italy appeared to be incapable of escaping past practice of funding growth largely out of debts. But the days of available, cheap capital were long gone. The drive to improve plant, to better and expand the product range, was thus continually hampered by a decrepit financial structure. True, the government had in fact given quite considerable sums to Finsider—over 5,000 billion lire (mainly in the form of State endowment funds—*fondi di dotazione*) between 1976 and early 1983. The EEC, in an official document from mid-1983, stated that 'les interventions financières publiques décidées en sa faveur (la sidérurgie à participation d'Etat) sont—quelque soit le critère d'évaluation retenu—les plus importantes de la Communauté'.[27] But these capital injections were never sufficient to cover the desperate shortage of capital inherited from the boom years of the economic miracle. Moreover, they tended to come at irregular intervals, long after they were needed, in a last minute rush to pull Finsider back from the brink. They have therefore been inadequate for breaking the vicious debt circle in which public sector steel in Italy remains trapped.

ENTER THE CRISIS

The persistent troubles of the State steel sector, which gave no glimmer of improving, and the parlous state of public sector finances generally, began finally in the early Eighties to provoke a more widespread acceptance of the need for tough remedial action. For so long Italy had argued that it was a special case — that its industry was comparatively modern, and so it should not be made to carry out the sort of capacity cuts occuring north of the Alps. All that was needed were more funds. But as the projections of successive steel plans were swept aside by the deepening recession, and Finsider's oft-promised return to financial health remained as elusive as ever, it became increasingly difficult to evade a growing realisation that public sector steel in Italy was in need of more than just money. And in any case the sort of sums being requested — the 1983 plan suggested that 5,000 billion lire were needed to restore Finsider to health by 1985 — simply bore no relation to the State's financing capabilities.

The size of the public sector deficit in Italy had reached 16 per cent of GDP by 1983, while the public debt took up 81 per cent of GDP compared with an average of 51 per cent for the seven OECD countries. Worse still, the public sector deficit gave every sign of breaking the psychologically important barrier of 100,000 billion lire in 1984, threatening both to create a potentially grave source of instabililty within the Italian economy, and to undermine Italy's international credibility. The Governor of the Bank of Italy, Carlo Azeglio Ciampi, repeatedly issued stern warnings about the urgent need to control State spending. In late 1983 the IMF added its voice to the growing chorus of concern, cautioning that Italy was sitting on a time-bomb, which threatened the very stability of its economic system.

The finances of IRI itself were in a deplorable state. From 103 billion in 1974, IRI's losses rose relentlessly to reach 2,800 billion lire by 1982, while the accumulated debt exceeded turnover. Its debt servicing charges had reached 17 per cent of turnover (against a private sector average of 3,5 per cent). Responsible for over two thirds of IRI's losses, Finsider stood out as the prime guilty party. In seeking to stem the loss of State funds, attention therefore focused on improving the balance sheets in public sector steel. In October 1982 Confindustria — the employers' federation — argued that the capacity cuts being urged on Finsider by the EEC commission ought to be accepted 'con la consapevolezza che è questo l'unico modo per evitare crisi ancora più profonde e preoccupanti'. [28] By the summer of 1983 Romano Prodi, the President of IRI, was stating bluntly that Finsider needed 'a Fiat cure', referring to the substantial reductions in manning levels carried out by Turin motor manufacturer in the early Eighties. The prospect of plant closures was considered by a growing number to be unavoidable.

Just as the future of public sector steel was undergoing reappraisal inside Italy, so growing pressure was being exerted from outside. In Brussels irritation was rising with Italy's continued claim be be a special case for exemption from the crisis regime imposed by the EEC Commission after October 1980. Consumption in Italy was no longer pulling ahead as in the past, while the steel firms' mounting losses, with several steelworks operating at well below economically viable capacity levels, only reinforced the Commission's determination to impose capacity cuts on Finsider. Those other EEC countries which had already pushed through harsh restructuring programmes, often at great political cost, were reluctant to see Italy being treated differently. In mid-1983 the Commission issued a virtual ultimatum — 4.8 million tonnes of public sector steelmaking capacity (plus 1 million tonne in private sector) had to be cut, in an effort to reduce Italy's total capacity to 30 million tonnes by 1986.

After an initial period of blustering, the Italian government recognised, if belatedly, that radical action would indeed have to be taken. As if to drive the point home, Romano Prodi urged the steel industry to shed some 25,000 jobs as quickly as possible.

This greater willingness to adopt a strategy of crisis managment in steel also reflected in part the much reduced power of the trade unions. In the early stages of this chapter the strength of organised labour was cited as one of the main elements explaining the continued growth of the State steel sector, even after the international prospects for the steel industry had turned distinctly gloomy. Management's inability seriously to contemplate slimming down the labour force, despite some obvious areas of overmanning, stemmed in part from a virtual veto on labour policy wielded by the trade unions. This power, however, was dealt a body blow during the 40 days at Fiat in October 1980 when the Communist party and the main unions suffered a humiliating defeat (they were disowned by much of the workforce itself) in their effort to maintain employment levels at all cost. The tide had begun to turn perceptibly against the unions. By the end of 1982 the FLM's membership had declined to the 1971 level of less than 850,000. Even though the sort of mass redundancies seen in northern Europe have not yet been attempted in Italy, the increasing use of the *cassa integrazione* — often at the rate of 100 per cent — in combination with early retirement, has effectively achieved similar results.

A reluctance to administer job losses was still, however, much in evidence. The Italian govenment cast around for ways of minimising the impact of the cuts demanded by the EEC. The dilemma that all parties concerned — politicians, unionists, industrialists — strove to circumvent, was having to choose between either Bagnoli or Cornigliano. Both were heavy loss makers, and in recent years had been operating at low capacity, when not actually closed. Brussels, in particular, made it quite clear that it wanted the shutdown of one or the other. But the whole weight of the State assistential tradition, of the concern to preserve jobs in the South, and of the persistent view of steel as a key component in Italy's industrial survival, all militated against making such drastic choices. The efforts of the revised steel plan in 1984 to redistribute the costs of contraction across both the public and the private sectors, with a decision to introduce early retirement at fifty as the only way of reducing the workforce by the numbers required (26,500), reflected the continuing desire to reconcile economic necessity with the preservation of social harmony.

At the end of October 1984 an agreement was finally reached whereby part of the Cornigliano works was taken over by a consortium of private industrialists, the COGEA. With an estimated production of just 600 m.t. in 1985 — long laminates — only 1,600 workers were to be kept on. At Bagnoli, originally scheduled to reopen in 1983, the modernised plant continued to limp in late 1984 towards the resumption of production. Throughout the summer the factory council had resisted tooth and nail the accord signed in May by the national union confederations and Italsider on early retirement and reopening the works. In an effort to solve the deadlock, a referendum was held in July, and a substantial majority of those who voted disavowed their hardline local representatives in favour of the original May agreement. The works were, at the time of writing, to reopen with about 4,200 employees, but it is generally accepted that even this reduced total will decline to around 3,000 by 1986. The referendum was, indeed, a remarkable event, indicating how far the climate on the shop floor had changed. The first referendum in a major Italian firm had been won — comfortably — by the advocates of modernisation, in this case the reformist wing of the Neapolitan PCI. In itself, the signing of the national agreement on early retirement — which IRI and Finsider felt to be the most convenient way of achieving the desired number of job losses without redundancies — marked a considerable evolution in trade union thinking. In just the first eight months of 1984, some 10,000 jobs were cut. Between 1982 and late 1984 Finsider had shed some 16,000 posts, supplemented in 1983 alone, by the use of *cassa integrazione* for an average of 13,000 workers. What only a few years previously was a revolutionary break with past labour practices initiated by the private Fiat corporation, has with unforseen rapidity, been accepted by the public sector. Nevertheless, these attempts to cushion the impact of the job losses will prove to be enormously costly, despite EEC assistance. Much enthusiastic talk during the summer of 1984 about creating an emergency regime for the worst hit areas (Genoa, Naples, Sardinia, the so-called *bacini di crisi*) disappeared into the abyss separating rhetoric from reality. De Michelis, Minister for Labour in the Craxi government, also spoke of creating some 100,000 jobs in the public sector, especially in the economically deprived areas. Such well-intentioned musings were met with a characteristically stony silence by those holding the purse strings.

As a final point it is worth returning to the observation with which this chapter began. Italy's steel industry gained world stature during a time of boom; it achieved greatness at a time of crisis. Is this evidence of the superiority of muddling through? Has the Italian public steel sector, despite the contradictions, inconsistencies, broken promises and unmet deadlines, bureaucratic blunders and political interference, succeeded where others, apparently more ordered, coherent and focused, have failed? In part, the answer is yes. For if Italy had had a disciplined, accountable government, with a coherent industrial policy, and if IRI had operated according to the dictates of a responsible financial policy, and had based its actions on a more rigorous interpretation of economic conditions, then the Italian public sector steel industry would never have developed as it did up until the early Eighties. Rather, like most of its competitors, it most probably would have contracted. It was the uncoordinated nature of policy, the fractures between and within the government and industry, that permitted such prodigious structures to be built on such precarious foundations. How the bill for such profligacy will eventually be paid remains the crucial question.

NOTES

1 For a more detailed analysis cf. J. Eisenhammer and M. Rhodes, 'The Politics of Public Sector Steel in Italy: From the economic miracle to the crisis of the eighties' — *The Western European Steel Project,* European University Institute, Florence. Forthcoming.

2 Cf. *Prospettive e Problemi della Siderurgia Italiana,* Associazione Industrie Siderurgiche Italiane (Assider), June 1980, p. III. (Hereafter referred to as Assider Report 1980)

3 G. Bocca, 'L'avventura dell'acciaio, Part II', in *La Repubblica,* 16 July 1983.

4 G. De Michelis et al. *Rapporto sulle Partecipazioni Statali,* F. Angelis, Milano, 1981, pp 0-157.

5 Assider Report, op. cit., pp. 36-37; R. A. Sabatino, 'Problems of the Italian Steel Industry' in ADEFI, *Les Restructurations industrielles en France,* Economica, Paris, 1980, p. 105.

6 Cf. M. de Gaspari, 'Il crack dell'altoforno', *Mondo Economico,* 18 March 1981.

7 *Programma Finalizzato Industria Siderurgica,* Ministero dell'Industria, del Commercio e dell'Artigianato, Roma, 1979. p. 72. (Hereafter referred to as 1979 Steel Plan)

8 Figures given in the 1979 Steel Plan, p. 50.

9 1979 Steel Plan, p. 125; Sabatino, op. cit., p. 112.

10 Cited in *La Stampa,* 20 October 1977.

11 Cited in *Mondo Economico,* 29 July 1978.

12 For example see the 1979 Steel Plan, p. 117. This was certainly the argument used in the late Seventies by the then Minister for State Participation, Sino Lombardini, to convince the EEC of the need to redevelop Italsider-Bagnoli.

13 Between 1974 and 1980, while steel consumption in the rest of Europe dropped by 16% in Italy it rose by 12%.

14 The 1979 Steel Plan, p. 21.

15 Loc. Cit. pp. 79-80.

16 Loc. Cit., p. 75.

17 Loc. Cit., p. 98.

18 Cf. The speech by Pietro Armani, Vice-President of IRI, reprinted in *Mondo Economico,* 13 December 1980.

19 Assider Report, 1980, p. 18.

20 *Piano della Siderurgia a Partecipazione Statale,* Rome, 1981. (Hereafter referred to as the 1981 CIPI Plan)

21 Cited in *Il Sole-24 Ore,* 17 October 1980.

22 1981 CIPI Plan, p. 63.

23 Loc. Cit., p. 49.

24 Loc. Cit., p. 9 and p. 61.

25 Cf. *Mondo Economico,* 4 March, 1981.

26 This situation was not limited to the State steel sector alone. In the period 1973-1979, self-financing covered on average only 8 per cent of gross investment by public enterprises, *Annals of Public and Cooperative Economy,* 1 March 1982, p. 10.

27 *Tageblatt* (Luxembourg), 13 July 1983.

28 Cited in *Il Sole-24 Ore,* 8 October 1982.

THE CHANGING ROLE OF THE VATICAN IN ITALIAN POLITICS

Paul Furlong

> I want to make clear my thinking with an image: in the piazza in front of a church meet those who come out of the church sanctified, those who are going into the church to sanctify themselves, and others who stop in the square to engage in business or in conversation; even these from time to time raise their eyes to the church, as if they wished they had the time or the leisure or the will to enter.
> The political party can be likened to the crowd in the piazza; they cannot avoid seeing the church from whichever route they arrive there.[1]

In 1944 the Italian Catholic priest, Don Luigi Sturzo, could envisage a Christian Democrat Party whose relationship with the Church had clear boundaries and stable communication routes. The relationship that actually developed in the post-war period lacked these, and while one should not over-stretch his metaphor, the problems that rapidly emerged can be described within the same image: firstly that the Church, and in particular Pius XII, Pope from 1939 to 1958, claimed the right not only to sanctify those within the building but also to sanctify the entire piazza; and secondly, that though they might not be able to avoid seeing the church many of those within the piazza had no wish to enter it whatsoever.

From the outset, therefore, the relationship was a difficult one. As has been argued elsewhere,[2] in the early post-war period Pius XII adopted a strategy of mobilisation and commitment of Catholic laity through a variety of national associations such as Catholic Action (AC), the Association of Italian Catholic Workers (ACLI), and Civic Committees; if he was concerned over the possible threat which might come from the Communists and Socialists to the Church's interests protected in the Concordat, he was also eager to extend the institutional authority of the Church within Italy, to impress Catholic morality onto the soft clay of the new political system, and to integrate Catholics into the political life in the country. But the chosen instruments for these operations were

intended to be under the close control of the Church, and this did not
exclude the Christian Democrat Party, which Pius XII seems to have seen
as the party for all Catholics and for Catholics exclusively. This strategy,
and these means of carrying it out, were not arrived at simplistically, nor
were they the only possible options. Another plausible outcome which at
least appeared in the debates in Catholic circles was the possible survival
of a plurality of Catholic political organisations, including Catholic
-Socialist and even Catholic-Communist ones. This was never a strong
contender, particularly in view of the treatment of Catholics in the Soviet
Union, which was a matter of grave concern to Pius XII. Another factor
which weighed against plurality was that the existence of more than one
Catholic party would seriously weaken Catholic lay influence within the
system as a whole because of fragmentation of the Catholic vote. Not
least, it would be very difficult for the Pope and the hierarchy to insist on
a single message carrying the Church's authority in such circumstances.
It appears also that the Vatican gave serious consideration to tacit or
explicit support for the establishment of an authoritarian, possibly
monarchist, political regime in post-war Italy, but there were strong
tactical arguments against this.[3] The Church in principle was committed
to no one political system but held itself to offer a third way between
capitalism and socialism. In the event, however, the Church's support
for a single Catholic party within a liberal-democratic political system
was a crucial factor in legitimising the new post-war Republican regime.
    There were several major consequences for the new regime. The most
obvious was that the new party found a unifying factor in anti-
Communism, one of the very few specific and applicable policies the
Church's social doctrine could be held to imply which would be readily
acceptable to a majority in the party. The expulsion of the PCI from the
governing coalition in May 1947, and the veto on its future participation,
was part of the process by which the liberal-democratic regime acquired
a more moderate cast than its relatively radical Constitution might have
implied. Another major consequence lay in the way in which the DC
attempted to resolve the problem of its relationship with the Church.
The Church's support for the DC as the sole expression of Catholic
interest was crucial to the DC's development as the largest single party,
but the party that developed was neither the pliant instrument of the
Church envisioned by Pius XII nor the meeting-place of plural interests
inspired and united by Catholic morality, as described by Sturzo. The
construction of an independent party organisation which would not rely
on the Civic Committees was a priority both of Alcide De Gasperi, the
first post-war DC Prime Minister, and of Amintore Fanfani, who became
Party Secretary in 1954. Both under Fanfani, and after his resignation in

1959, the DC developed a party organisation which relied not on the constraining influence of the Church but on the DC's control of major spending ministries in government, on connections with the expanding public sector, on direct links with Catholic occupational groups such as Coldiretti, and not least on its appeal to conservative lay voters. These developments served not to exclude the Vatican and the bishops from the political sphere, but rather to increase the ambiguity about the role of the Church in Italian politics: the DC remained the privileged interlocutor of the Church, recruited heavily among the Catholic associations, and continued to talk of itself as a Catholic party, even as its organisation and its policies led it towards an identity composed of an enigmatic mix of clientelism and technocracy, of Catholicism and conservative liberalism, of governmental power bases and entrenched local party chieftains.

But the Church was also developing an awareness of changed external circumstances and new interpretations of its own needs. The Second Vatican Council, held in Rome from 1962 to 1965, gave wide currency and increased legitimacy to a variety of themes associated with the *aggiornamento*, the bringing up to date and renewal of the Church's structures. Among the themes which most affected the Church in Italian politics were a new emphasis on the responsibility of the bishops as successors of the Apostles, concern for the international nature of the Church's mission, and a tolerance of the beliefs of non-Christians and of non-Catholic Christians.

The pontificate of Paul VI from 1963 to 1978 was characterised for much of its duration by an increasing disengagement of the Papacy from direct intervention in Italian politics. Pope Pius XII frequently referred directly, and with authority, to details of Italian political life, and Italian bishops, given such a strong lead and the conformism inherent in the traditional view of their function, echoed his views dutifully and with very little public deviation. Paul VI came to papal office with a reputation as a genuine Conciliar bishop, committed to the implementation of the Council's decrees; while there may be much to debate in other quarters about his successes or failings in terms of the international cohesion of the Church, liturgical reform, reform of the Curia, and other matters relating to the Church's internal organisation, there can be little dispute that the impact of his pontificate in Italian politics resulted in a decrease in the number of papal interventions and a considerable change in their tone and substance. The Vatican at least appeared willing to recognise the new role of the Church in what had become a largely secularised society; both formally and practically, this meant a greater pastoral role for the bishops within an enhanced collegial body, the Italian Bishops Conference (CEI). However, the bishops themselves showed greater inertia and for much of Paul's pontificate patently failed to provide the kind of pastoral authority required of them by the Council. They, perhaps more than any other sector of the Church in Italy, failed to show in their dispositions and behaviour the flexible awareness of the decline in the Church's influence. This should not be surprising, granted their origins, background and rigid training, though it should also be observed that the rejuvenation of the domestic Italian Church was hampered by the incompleteness of Paul VI's attempts to reform the Curia, which is the Vatican bureaucracy. A particular example is the appointment of leading conservatives, Carlo Confalonieri and then in 1973 Sebastiano Baggio, to head the Congregation of Bishops; it would be wrong to attribute too much to the power of individuals, but certainly the pattern of appointments of bishops in Italy during Paul VI's reign was characterised by administrative caution, promoting loyalty and experience rather than capacity for dynamic renewal.[4]

In keeping with this pattern, there has been a tendency in the Italian Church, as in Italian society, towards a greater uniformity and national standardisation. But this process is still a minor theme appearing in counterpoint to the major characteristic which modulates any generalisation about Italian politics, that is, regional and hierarchical differentiation. This has important effects on the authority of the Church at the local level, and it does not occur only in the administrative area. It is clear that secularisation has had a strong national impact, in association with the very rapid socio-economic and demographic change since the early 1950s, but the increase in areligiosity is not visible in all areas equally—there is an immediately recognisable difference in religious culture between a parish in a suburb of Milan in the urbanised industrial North, and a parish in a suburb of Naples, for example;[5] and research produces examples that differ markedly from both of those areas in terms of level of religious attendance and in terms of institutional and collective patterns of religious behaviour.[6] This regional differentiation occurs with hierarchical differentiation also, which affects both the Church and the Christian Democrat Party.

To restate what is perhaps obvious, if sometimes neglected, the Vatican is not identical with the Catholic Church. The Vatican is not merely a synthesis of over one hundred national Churches, nor does it exercise total reflexive command over the individual national Churches, not even the Italian one. The growing difference between the concerns of the Vatican and the concerns of the Italian Catholic hierarchy is one of the major developments in this area in recent years, though this is more visible after the pontificate of Paul VI than during it. The conformation to be considered is not therefore a simple triangular one comprising the Catholic Church, the Christian Democrat Party and the electorate, but a much more complex shape involving regional differentiation in all three and relatively autonomous institutional units within the first two. In referring to the secularisation of the Christian Democrat Party, we should not ignore the fact that in many areas, particularly in the North, the DC still relies heavily on activists drawn into the party from Catholic associations, mixing as it still does a prosperous conservative appearance with a more inter-class, religious and populist one.[7] Personal links between Vatican officials or residential bishops and senior members of the Christian Democrat Party remained strong during Paul VI's pontificate; there was a long-established relationship between Paul VI himself and the DC leaders Aldo Moro and Giulio Andreotti which dated from Paul VI's position, early in his career, as national chaplain to the Italian Catholic Graduates Association (FUCI). The relationship between the Church and the DC therefore, though changing in intensity and importance, rested on a variety of channels of communication and retained sporadic vigour. But both in the Vatican and in the Italian hierarchy, the new groups which were emerging among Catholic laity, such as *Comunione e Liberazione* (CL), were increasingly favoured as an alternative form of political leverage.

The process of disengagement from Italian politics moderated during the latter part of Paul VI's reign, perhaps as a result of the defeat of the Catholic anti-divorce campaign in the divorce referendum of 1974[8] and a certain disillusion with the lack of leadership in the Italian bishops; but also the Pope showed great concern for the general heightening of social tensions, the increase in terrorism and the severe economic problems after the 1973 oil shock. The electoral surge of the PCI in 1975 and 1976 was also a mattter which prompted his intervention. In the 1976 election campaign Paul VI intervened with relative directness and force to warn Catholics of the dangers of Communism,[9] and in the period before his death, which came in August 1978, he was more vocal than in the past, commenting on various crises as they occurred and curtailing though not eliminating his usual acknowledgement of his position extraneous to Italian politics. In 1978 there were interventions on the Moro kidnapping, words of encouragement over the enforced resignation of President Leone, and, as we discuss later, warnings on the abortion law when it came into force. His congratulations to the new President, Sandro Pertini, had the ring of one who was welcoming a relative foreigner to a city which, though it might be the capital and place of residence of the new head of State belonged not to Italy but, through the Church, to the whole world.[10]

This does not mean however that the CEI and individual bishops were noticeably less active; on the contrary, as Paul VI took closer interest the CEI seemed to become more confident, denouncing Catholic-Communist agreement repeatedly. In the early 1960s, the benevolence of Giovanni Montini, then Archbishop of Milan, was a crucial factor in the establishment of a local Centre-Left coalition there, which set a major precedent for the national Centre-Left coalition later. In the mid-1970s, no such benevolence towards the historic compromise was forthcoming either from Giovanni Montini, as Pope Paul VI, or from the CEI. In November 1977 the permanent council of the CEI issued a firm statement, redolent of the early post-war utterances of Pius XII, which said among other things, 'The Christian faith and Marxism are irreconcilable in theory and in practice'.[11]

Until the Second Vatican Council, such a statement from such a source would have been unexceptional; twelve years after the end of the Council it marked a distinct attempt to reverse the trends within the Italian Church to the political pluralism which had been explicitly encouraged further, though not with reference to Marxism, in Paul VI's apostolic letter *Octogesima Adveniens*.[12] In early 1978, in the middle of difficult negotiations over the formation of a new government with PCI support, the CEI Annual Conference published a statement 'on the present difficulties', and unapologetically warned of their opposition to the PCI in terms which were unmistakeable (even if typically elliptical) in their reference to 'totalitarian and hegemonic planning'.[13]

There is a certain continuity between the approach of Paul VI in his later period, after 1975, and that of John Paul II, though of course the personal styles of the two Popes are very different indeed. The pastoral activism of the CEI is encouraged by John Paul II, but John Paul intervenes more frequently and more directly even than Pope Paul in his later years, and rarely troubles to place his remarks within the context of action already taken by the CEI. It is necessary therefore to look at his other statements and actions to determine the development of his general policy towards Italy. The central concept in his approach seems to be the idea of the Church as a universal institution with many national manifestations. The function of the Papacy is to express the universality of the Church, to guard its traditions and its authority, therefore, and to ensure that the national Churches maintain their doctrinal and institutional allegiance to the universal Church while giving recognition to their particular national or regional concerns. As a member of vigorous national Church prior to becoming Pope, John Paul's Christian experience was of a combative, hostile State confronting strong Catholic popular sentiments, which were closely associated with nationalism. In general he valued highly the national variations of Catholicism that result from faith being tested and surviving in particular cultures. At the same time, as a senior member of the Polish hierarchy, he showed himself capable of diplomacy and positive compromise in relations with the state authorities, and was less willing than Cardinal Wyczinski, then Primate of Poland, to seek confrontation.[14] As Pope, and having to deal with many different national problems, he has been careful to recognise the value of national autonomy, while at the same time establishing clearly his own right and obligation to intervene wherever he see deficiencies or weaknesses in the universal aspect of the national Churches' operations. His repeated references to the collegial dimension of his work are part of the same policy and derive directly from his commitment to implementation of the teachings of the Second Vatican Council on the place of the bishops in the Church.

Previous post-war Popes have had difficulty combining the different roles of the Papacy in international affairs with those forced on the institution by the very close historical ties with Italy. In the case of Pope Pius XII, the respect for national autonomy was little more than a decorous nod and collegiality was no more than a gleam in the eyes of suspect radical theologians. Paul VI showed great sensitivity for the separation of the Papacy from Italian affairs for much of his reign, but he never articulated clearly a coherent vision which might have enabled him to speak as Bishop of Rome. As we have seen, he sometimes appeared to regard the city of Rome as an extension of the universal Church rather than as a capital city of a nation-state. He therefore did not use his bishopric of Rome as a foothold in Italian society. In practice, he appears to have seen himself as an international Pope for whom the Italian connection was uncomfortable but unavoidable. For John Paul II the dual role of international religious leader and Bishop of Rome does not appear troublesome. His speeches to Italian audiences are strewn with references to his position as a stranger welcomed into a new home, but this seems to present itself to him as an extra opportunity, not as a limitation; instead of backing up his interventions on Italian politics with a carefully-manufactured acknowledgement of previous statements on the subject by the CEI or by the Cardinal-Vicar of Rome, John Paul appears content to refer to his position as Bishop of Rome in implicit justification.[15]

Paul VI travelled to an unprecedented extent, but his voyages always seemed to represent a special effort on his behalf, a privilege for the hosts, an extraordinary event. The travels of John Paul II certainly have the quality of extraordinary events, but that is because of his crowd-pulling capacity and his personal approach; there is nothing extraordinary about the countries he has visited—on the contrary he seems really to regard the entire world as his diocese and to be willing to visit wherever humanly possible. It is understandable that Paul VI should wish to visit the United Nations, the Middle East, or the Indian sub-continent, to take a special message to particularly important locations. But John Paul seems to wish to visit countries that have no great claims to strategic importance in the Catholic world, such as Britain, as well as the sensitive areas, which he certainly is determined to visit also. In each country he seems to find a national message for Catholics. In the developed West, this message is usually a national version of a severe warning against the dangers of consumerism and obsession with material things: in this he tries to present himself as the voice of the authentic traditions of national Catholicism. In Ireland, for example, he proclaimed that the Irish nation was at a turning point in its development and could choose either to be true to its Catholic traditions or to pursue the hedonistic path of developed Western societies. 'The voice of your ancestors speaks through me,' he told an enormous and perhaps startled congregation at Limerick in October 1979.[16] It would be misleading to describe John Paul II as a fundamentalist; though the robustness and intensity of his statements sometimes might suggest a simplicity of approach, his teaching is far from simple and his general strategy appears to be guided by a conservative interpretation of the teachings of the Second Vatican Council, to whose implementation, however, he is firmly committed. Indeed, on an issue like the collegiality of bishops with the Pope, he can appear, as did Paul VI in Italy, rather more progressive than the bishops of the countries which he visits.[17]

Italy presents its own problems for the Vatican—divorce and abortion legislation, the revision of the Concordat, and links between the Vatican Bank (IOR) and suspect Italian financiers are major issues demanding attention at the highest level. John Paul's approach in Italy is not fundamentally divergent from his general strategy elsewhere, with the important exception that his position as Bishop of Rome is used to allow him a direct voice and national pastoral responsibility here, as well as the functions inherent in his role as universal pastor. In addition to his claim to represent to national Churches the traditions and eternal authority of the universal Church, there is this further dimension which makes his involvement in Italian affairs more frequent, more direct, and more detailed than elsewhere. The fact that he is a non-Italian has not diminished the activity of the Papacy in Italy—on the contrary, it appears to have freed this Pope from the weight of historical conventions by which some previous Popes apparently have felt bound. Whether his lack of detailed previous experience of Italian politics makes him more clumsy and maladroit than his predecessors is more debatable. Whatever may be thought of the content of his interventions, his approach has a coherence and a logic to it which might make it easier for his successors to follow, than were the almost obsessive concern for the *minutiae* of Italian politics, characteristic of Pius XII, or the anxious sensitivity of the early years of Paul VI for the formal separation of the Papacy from the responsibilities of the Bishop of Rome. The collegial relationship with the national bishops is, therefore, qualitatively different and closer here. John Paul II expressed his relationship with the Italian Church clearly in his speech to the annual meeting of the CEI in 1980:

> Yes, brothers, we are the bishops of the Church in Italy, we have received from God this enormous and exalting responsibility: you who have been brought into the ranks of the successors of the Apostolic College to be the spiritual guides of the Italian people, to which you belong by birth, by disposition, by education, by social and religious culture, and from which you have been drawn to fulfil your mission; I who, although coming from another nation, have become by unfathomable divine wish Bishop of Rome, successor of Peter in the see of Rome. So I have received this primacy in virtue of which I have a specific mandate as Vicar of Christ and Pastor of the Universal Church, without on that account forgetting the very particular solicitude, the links and the commitments which the care of my diocese of Rome requires.[18]

The Pope then went on to refer to his visits to dioceses around Italy and his interest in his diocese of Rome in terms which were clearly intended to encourage the bishops to see him as a co-worker with them. In his capacity to affirm and reinforce the activity of the local Churches John Paul II appears a charismatic leader unlike any of his immediate predecessors other than John XXIII, and he has undoubtedly given confidence both to the CEI and to the new lay groups, though as was observed earlier, the Italian Church had begun to stretch itself even before his election.

But the intentions and motivations of the Pope are only part of the explanation of the role of the Vatican, of the Church and more generally of religious belief in Italian politics. The major development in Italy which demanded John-Paul's attention in the early years of his pontificate was the emergence and persistence of the abortion issue; it is worth considering in some detail the travails which attended this issue for the light they throw both on the policy-making process and on the difficult relationship between the DC and the Church.

As was the case with the other major reforms of the period, the impetus to abortion reform did not come directly from the governing parties as such and in no way from the DC, who opposed this reform. Signatures for referendums on abortion, and other issues, were first collected successfully by the Radical Party in 1975, which wanted the repeal of the relevant section of the Penal Code; this would have had the effect of decriminalising and entirely deregulating abortion.

The referendums should then have been held in the second quarter of 1976; lay parties attempted to avoid the abortion referendum by proposing bills in parliament regulating and decriminalising abortion, but in April 1976 the joint lay proposal was amended successfully by the Christian Democrats to restrict abortion to cases of rape or where the mother's life was directly at risk. This amendment was passed with the support of the neo-Fascist party, the MSI, which made it even more unacceptable to the lay parties. The resulting law would not have been sufficient to prevent the referendum, but the referendum was avoided on this occasion in the same way as the first proposed referendum had been in 1972; on that occasion the collapse of the governmental coalition ensued from, among other things, the controversy over the divorce law, and resulted in the dissolution of parliament and the calling of early parliamentary elections. Because of the intervals of time demanded in the 1970 Referendum Law, the divorce referendum could not be held until 14 May 1974, nearly two years after the previous parliamentary elections. In the case of the abortion referendum, similar considerations applied, but on this occasion there was a narrow lay majority in parliament, which was not so in the 1972–1976 legislature. A further effort by the lay parties at an abortion law, which would render the referendum unnecessary, was passed by the Chamber of Deputies in January 1977, only to be defeated by two votes in the Senate in June 1977, when the absence of some Senators belonging to the smaller lay parties was crucial. The Christian Democrat position on the referendum was clear, if unhelpful: the abortion referendum was the responsibility of a lay movement, and while the DC claimed not to want the referendum to occur, they did not see it as their task to pass legislation decriminalising abortion, to which they were opposed in principle, for the purpose of avoiding the referendum. They were happy therefore to draw what profit they could from the discomfiture of the other parties and to demonstrate their own relative compactness over an issue which recalled them to their Catholic origins. If Aldo Moro, then Secretary of the DC, calculated that the PCI would be unwilling to withdraw support from the government over such an issue, then his calculations were correct. Abortion legislation, like divorce legislation previously, compelled the PCI to tread a difficult path between the threat to religious peace on the one side, and its radical lay principles on the other. On the other two issues that now looked likely to proceed to referendum, which were the Reale anti-terrorist law and the law on State finance for political parties, the PCI officially regretted the call for referendums, but it was not willing to support legislation to reform the laws in the direction required to avoid referendums. The abortion issue was very different: the original legislation was defended by virtually no one except the neo-Fascists, but merely to counsel a vote in favour of repeal would have left the Radicals as the spearhead of lay reform; also the PCI could not have been assured that it would be on the winning side; and if the Radical proposal were successful, the social consequences would have demanded legislation in any case.

Though the abortion issue did nothing to improve relations between the two major parties, it is an indication of the changed religious climate in Italy that the DC provided merely a passive obstruction on this major issue while the PCI did all they could to limit any wider repercussions. This attitude on the part of the DC was determined in long-range terms by the changes in origins and recruitment patterns of DC deputies and senators, which have rendered the Catholic associations and interest-groups much less influential than was the case even in the 1960s; but more specifically the political climate for religious issues was profoundly affected by the defeat of the anti-divorce lobby in 1974, which followed a vigorous and polemical campaign fought against divorce by the then DC party secretary Amintore Fanfani. While their position on the abortion issue might have been relatively comfortable in the short-term for the DC, it did have its costs in the long-term in the accelerating pace of the estrangement of the Catholic Church at various levels from the party which had once been regarded as its political offshoot. Catholic bishops and leading Catholic laity, in short, were not slow to grasp the implications of the DC's plea of diminished responsibility for what they saw as the very poor religious condition of the country.

The months that followed the defeat of the abortion bill in June 1977 were among the most difficult in the entire post-war period, mainly because of the continuing economic crisis and the very large increase in numbers of terrorist acts. In January 1978 the Andreotti government resigned after the withdrawal of PCI support; and when a new government was formed in March 1978, Aldo Moro was kidnapped by terrorists on the day of its presentation in parliament. The details of these developments do not concern us here; the events themselves help to explain why the abortion issue was not dealt with more rapidly, and why it seemed to be treated like a sporadically-remembered time-bomb ticking in the corner. After long delays, a new bill was passed by the Chamber of Deputies after a lengthy continuous sitting on 14 April

1978; the fiercest opposition was provided not by the DC but by the Radicals, who put down a total of 275 amendments and attempted to block the bill by filibuster, on the grounds that the bill did not liberalise abortion sufficiently. With unusual rapidity, the bill then went through the Senate unamended and was approved on 18 May 1978; it allowed termination of pregnancy on demand within the first 90 days and established a framework of medical and social support services to be provided free of charge. The new law came into effect on 1 June 1978, in time to avoid the referendum which had been formally called for 11 June.

The Italian hierarchy and Pope Paul VI did not speak in public on the issue during the legislative process, in deference to the separation of responsibilities, though the Catholic diocesan press, not subject to the same constraints, was more outspoken in its comments on the bill itself and on the political parties held responsible, including the DC. But once the law was in force, the full weight of the institutional Church's approval was voiced in public and at length, with statements from the CEI, from Cardinal Ugo Poletti, Vicar-General of the diocese of Rome, and finally from Pope Paul VI all within seven days of the new law's coming into operation.[19] In what was one of his last statements on Italian politics, Paul VI reiterated the unconditional claim of the Church to speak on such an issue as the interpreter of divine law and of natural law, and in his customary manner his statement was couched in terms of support for Poletti's statement. Cardinal Poletti had urged on Catholics involved in medical professions the duty of conscientious objection, which was allowed in the new law, and had described in detail how Catholics could register as conscientious objectors. This concern for pastoral practicalities is part of the Church's newly-changed role in Italian society. On issues such as divorce, the CEI had tended to argue the doctrinal case, but with increasing confidence in its pastoral role it has concerned itself with the organisation and direction of the Church's practical activity. In December 1978 the Permanent Council of the CEI published a document entitled 'Pastoral Instruction' on 'The Christian Community and the reception of new-born human life'. This ran to about ten thousand words, specified in detail the appropriate conduct of all categories of Catholics to the abortion law, ordered the establishment of a network of welfare services for families and for pregnant women, and in an unusually clear final paragraph on political commitment, called on all Catholics among other things

> to take action so that the present law, which is morally unacceptable, is replaced by legislation which fully respects the right to life.[20]

This was widely interpreted to mean that Catholics should call for a referendum on the issue. The CEI, again unusually, also had words in the same paragraph directly aimed at Catholics in Parliament, who were told that they were

> called to bear witness to their love of justice and to their disinterested concern for the true common good. Conscious of their responsibilities, they must not consider themselves dispensed from the moral duty to act to limit as far as possible the negative effects of the present law on abortion, and above all to replace it.[21]

For the next two and a half years, the Pope and the CEI lost few opportunities to emphasise their opposition to the new law, and were aided in this by the fact that 1980 was International Year of the Child.[22] But there was a distinct tendency to give prominence to the issue of freedom of conscience, an indication perhaps of their relative contentment with the campaign to encourage registration of conscientious objectors in the first 12 months of the law. Yet again, however, the pace was forced by the Radical Party, which began collecting signatures in 1980 for a referendum on the further liberalisation of abortion, along with other issues. It appears unlikely that without this the Church would have taken direct action, but this campaign by the Radicals was clearly felt to be a direct challenge to the Church; unless the Church promoted its own campaign for a return to a more strict law, it would be placed in the very difficult position of having to defend a law to which it had categorically and repeatedly stated its opposition. Signatures were collected by 'Movement for Life', a Catholic lay group, in the second quarter of 1980, with active support from the local churches, and the referendum was called for the same date as the Radical referendums, 17 May 1981.

The involvement of Pope John Paul II in the referendum campaign was vigorous, sustained, unprecedented and controversial. In the two months immediately preceding the referendum, he referred repeatedly not to the vote but rather to the issue of abortion as such: the Church's position, voiced by the CEI also, was one of total opposition to abortion. The CEI statement of 18 March 1981 therefore criticised the Movement for Life proposal because it would allow therapeutic abortion. Nevertheless the proposal was described as 'morally licit' and a serious obligation was placed on Catholics to support it.[23] The Pope's statements, particularly one made at Bergamo on 26 April 1981, were widely criticised as an interference in the internal affairs of Italy, but as we have observed, the Pope's strategy is consistently interventionist not only in Italy but also wherever he sees fit—in effect marking a return to the absolute universal right of preaching the Gospel claimed by Pius XII, though in a rather more populist style.[24]

The Catholic referendum was defeated on a turnout of 79.6%, with 32.1% in favour and 67.9% against. The Church had the small but not insignificant compensation of seeing the Radical Party proposal defeated far more heavily, with 11.5% in favour and 88.5% against. This could not obscure the very striking fall in what may be fairly called the 'Catholic' vote from 42.1% on the issue of divorce in 1974, a decrease made all the more significant by the much greater efforts of the Church in 1981, by the much greater seriousness of the issue of abortion in Catholic doctrine, and by the uniformity of the defeat over the whole country. The only region to produce a majority against abortion was the German-speaking area of South Tirol on the northern borders with Austria. The South of Italy, which in 1974 had given small majorities against divorce in every region, and which is usually associated with highly traditional forms of Catholicism, showed a considerable swing against the Church's position. It is probable that this was a single-issue vote in the South, as the decline in the DC vote in the 1983 elections in the area was not so marked. The general conclusion to be drawn may be that just as the Church is coming to an appreciation of the weakness of the DC in policy areas related to religious issues, so the DC, whose leaders were relatively quiet during the abortion campaign, is making its own judgments about the capacity of electoral mobilisation of the Church.

There is not space here to discuss in detail other major issues in Vatican-Italian politics; but it must be observed that one effect of the resolution of the abortion issue was to unblock the negotiations over the revision of the Concordat, which had been initiated by the Italian Parliament in 1966. Under the chairmanship of one of the first-generation DC leaders, Guido Gonella, the revision had proceeded extremely slowly, with major delays over issues such as divorce and abortion. It may be understood as a corroboration of what we have argued here that on 18 February 1984 the new agreement was signed not by a Christian Democrat but by a Socialist Prime Minister, Bettino Craxi; the agreement was reached where others had failed over a period of 18 years by the simple expedient of excluding both the Italian parliament and the Bishops from having any powers over the detail of the negotiations. In effect the new Concordat was a general scheme of understanding, with several issues such as ecclesiastical property and regulations for religious teaching in schools left to negotiation by a specially-established joint commission between the Vatican and the Italian government. Apart from new agreements over salaries to clergy, over marriage law and in general terms over religious teaching, the new Concordat excluded any suggestion that Catholicism could be regarded as the religion of the State, as it had been in the 1929 Concordat. For the Italian government, the motivation and the gains were therefore clear; for the Vatican, on the other hand, the motivation was in the need to achieve a long-term settlement of the anomalies in the 1929 Concordat, preferably prior to further unfortunate revelations about the Vatican Bank. But also the new Concordat indicates a significant downgrading of the Italian arena in the Vatican's priorities, if the Vatican can view the loss of major privileges relating to taxation and to religious teaching with relative equanimity.

The Concordat also showed clearly how different now are the priorities of the Vatican from those sought by the Italian bishops. They were quick to argue, in a statement published on the day of the signing of the agreement, that the new Concordat did not adequately recognise the involvement of the Italian Church in new social problems 'such as the promotion of life, health, education, and the fight against new forms of exploitation'.[25] The new Concordat was criticised therefore as too much modelled on the old, oriented too narrowly towards the juridical problems associated with 'historical privileges' and not sufficiently towards 'modern realities'. The bishops also aimed barbed comments at the absence of any reference to Catholicism as the religion of the State, and at the changes in the provisions on marriage law. The comment from the DC was muted, but the conduct and outcome of the negotiations undoubtedly increased the distance between the Church and its traditional close ally. Particularly in lay circles, and in the Vatican, the success of the negotiations redounded strongly and favourably on the reputation of the Socialist Prime Minister, Bettino Craxi, after a long period of futile negotiations led by DC-controlled governments or by DC-controlled parliamentary commissions; but in the eyes of the Catholic bishops and of some laity, the DC stood accused implicitly yet again of not having been sufficiently active in furthering the interests of Catholicism in Italy.

In conclusion, it must be observed that while those involved in Italian politics at any level 'cannot', in Sturzo's terms, 'avoid seeing the Church', the Church itself does not give Italy the priority evident in the early post-war years; the priorities now are international to an extent unprecedented for many years. Vatican policy now bears the stamp of a Polish Pope who certainly does not ignore Italy but who has shown himself to have a distinctive set of aims for the Church. We have argued here against the view that Pope John Paul II is a simple fundamentalist with a successful populist style. On social and welfare issues, he speaks

with a genuine concern on behalf of those whom he sees as the poor and
the oppressed, while in matters of doctrine he is firmly traditional and
conservative — the anti-Communism which may have made him
acceptable at the time of his election is therefore more complex than that
of Pius XII, but it is no less severe on differences of principle. Though the
Pope may acknowledge responsibility to no temporal authority, he
certainly relies on temporal powers, and in particular on the Vatican's
Curia and the national bishops' conferences, to implement his policies,
and there are serious limitations on what he may achieve, in Italy as
elsewhere. John Paul's reform of the Curia in April 1984 appears to have
had the aim not of making the Curia more effectively answerable to him
but rather that of giving the Pope greater freedom from the cares of
bureaucracy, to enable him to fulfil his mission as Universal Pastor, by
increasing the powers of his Secretary of State. In further internationalis-
ing the Curia, however, he increased its heterogeneity and diversity and
appears to have allowed it to some extent a more ambiguous voice. One
of the results of this failure fully to control the Curia has been that the
Curia does not fully express the Pope's positive attitudes either towards
the teachings of the Second Vatican Council or towards pluralistic
national manifestations of Catholicism. Another constraint is that the
Pope's own concern to express and reinforce a unifying authority in the
Church conflicts with his belief in the collegiality of the Church's
decision-making. These problems have tended to weaken the role of the
Synod of Bishops, whose periodic meetings in Rome have so far failed to
fulfil the hopes of many progressive Conciliar bishops; another result has
been that in the face of continued national deviations from Papal
teachings on a variety of issues such as Marxism, birth control, and the
political role of the clergy, the Curia has either been driven back to or has
willingly re-adopted its centralising and standardising role. The impact
in Italy, as we have seen, is that the institutional Church as a whole now
relies more than previously on lay groups which it can control with
relative directness rather than on the DC or on formal Catholic
associations, and appears set on a conservative and anti-Communist
path.

NOTES

1 *Scritti politici di Luigi Sturzo*, introduzione a cura di Mario G. Rossi, Feltrinelli
   Editore, Milano, 1982, p. 366.
   Unless otherwise indicated, all translations in this essay are by the author.

2   See P.F. Furlong, *The Italian Christian Democrats, from Catholic Movement to conservative party*, Hull Papers in Politics, No. 26, University of Hull, 1982.

3   On the considerations behind these choices and the events that transpired, see D. Settembrini, *La Chiesa nella politica italiana (1944–1963)*, Biblioteca Universale Rizzoli, Milano, 1977.

4   See P.F. Furlong, *The Structure of the Catholic Church and its Political Predispositions in Italy* (unpublished paper 1976).

5   See G. Bussetti, et al. *Religione alla periferia*, Bologna, il Mulino, 1974; S. Burgalassi, *Il Comportamento Religiosi degli Italiani*, Vallecchi Editore, Firenze, 1968; and A. Pace, *L'uomo dei campi alla svolta dei tempi*, Casa Editrice d'Auria, Napoli, 1974.

6   See particularly S. Burgalassi, 1974, parts I and II; S.S. Acquaviva, 'Un primo contributo all sociologia storico-religiosa del padovano' pp. 86–97 in *Sociologia Religiosa*, vv. 5–6, 1960; S.S. Acquaviva, G. Guizzardi and G. Milanesie, 'Nouvelles formes de religiosité et developpement en Italie', pp. 157–181 in *Proceedings of 13th Conference on the Sociology of Religion, Religion and Social Change*, Lille, CISR, 1975.

7   In the now considerable literature on the DC, see A. Parisi (ed.), *Democristiani*, Il Mulino, Bologna, 1979; and G. Pasquino, 'Italian Christian Democracy — a party for all seasons', *West European Politics*, October 1979.

8   See P. F. Furlong, 'On millstones and milestones: the Italian Catholic hierarchy and the Divorce Referendum, May 1974' (Paper presented at the ECPR Joint Workshop Sessions, Workshop on 'Religion and Politics', Brussels 1979).

9   See *La Documentation Catholique*, June 1976, Vol. 73, No. 1569, pp. 501–502.

10   See *La Documentation Catholique*, August 1978, Vol. 75, No. 1747, p. 733.

11   *La Documentation Catholique*, January 1978, Vol. 75, No. 1733, p.43.

12   See especially para. 50, p. 38 in 'Octogesima Adveniens', Apostolic letter of Pope Paul VI, Catholic Truth Society, London, 1971.

13   *La Documentation Catholique*, February 1978, Vol. 75, No. 1736, pp. 177–179.

14   On John Paul's earlier career, see P. Hebblethwaite, *The Year of the Three Popes*, Collins, London, 1978, pp. 146–211.

15   See, for example, his sermon given on 5 November 1978 on St Francis of Assisi, in *La Documentation Catholique*, November 1978, Vol. 75, No. 1752, and his speech to the Permanent Council of the CEI on 23 January 1979, in *La Documentation Catholique*, March 1979, Vol. 76, No. 1759.

16   *La Documentation Catholique*, October 1979, Vol. 76, No. 1772, p. 867.

17   For an interpretation of his visit to Britain in this sense, see A. White, 'Dismantling the monolith — a retrospective view of the Papal visit', pp. 252–260 in *New Blackfriars*, June 1983.

18   *La Documentation Catholique*, July 1980, Vol. 77, No. 1790, p. 678.

19   Respectively, pp. 632, 630–632, and 605 in *La Documentation Catholique* July 1978, Vol. 75, No. 1745.

20   *La Documentation Catholique*, March 1979, Vol. 76, No. 1760, p.270.

21   *La Documentation Catholique*, March 1979, Vol. 76, No. 1760, p. 270.

22   *La Documentation Catholique*, Vols. 76 and 77, passim.

23   *La Documentation Catholique*, May 1981, Vol. 78, No. 1808, p. 460.

24   On this concept, see E. Troeltsch, *The Social Teachings of the Christian Churches*, v. 1, Allen and Unwin, London, 1931.

25   *La Repubblica*, Sunday, 19 February, 1984, p. 3; see also *L'Espresso*, 5 February 1984, p. 19.

MAKING SENSE OF ITALIAN COALITIONS

Geoffrey Pridham

WRITING over a decade ago, one observer of the Italian political scene composed a satire on coalitions in that country called 'Rules of the Crisis Game', in which he described the process of forming a government:

> The formalities of the masque. This is the grave second act. Rather than rolling up their sleeves and energetically giving the country a new government, the politicians bow to a form of protocol . . . . Moving with liturgical deliberateness, the Italian President consults for one week with all living former Presidents, all former Prime Ministers, all party leaders— including those of the extreme oppositions, even though they have no chance of being included in the next government. Since there have been 29 postwar Cabinets, the list of notables to be consulted grows longer with each year . . . The crisis is not over when the President designates the man most likely to succeed. This man will, anyway, accept the mandate 'with reservations', and then he begins his cycle of consultations, first with his own party and then with those parties which hopefully will join the coalition . . . These consultations, among men who have known each other's minds for 20 years, may be rather like a series of non-converging monologues. If the premier-designate has succeeded, he informs the President and then begins more consultations over the division of Cabinet seats and the Government's programme. When the premier-designate does not drop his 'reservations', the entire series of consultations begins again . . . .[1]

This certainly conveys a picture of elaborate procedures, leadership stagnation and the confusion that is widely attributed to the practice of Italian government.

Twelve years and seventeen governments later, this procedural scenario is still very familiar. There have been some changes, for Italy has since had a more resolute President than Leone (Pertini is accredited with preventing some governments collapsing through his direct intervention), some of the permanent fixtures on the political scene like Moro and Rumor have since departed (the one through assassination, the other through political disgrace) and some new faces have emerged such as Spadolini and Craxi, the first two non-Christian Democratic (DC) Prime Ministers since 1945. On the other hand, other old hands at the game of coalition politics have shown a remarkable durability. Fanfani surprised many with his return to the Palazzo Chigi, the seat of the head of government, in 1982 after an absence from that position of nearly twenty years, and then the following year Andreotti, several times Prime Minister in the 1970's and prior to that a Cabinet Minister in most governments ever since 1954, broke a four-year absence from high office with his appointment as Foreign Minister. While personalities might come and go — there has indeed been more changeover in prime ministerial and ministerial incumbency in recent years than was true in the 1950s and 1960s — one nevertheless feels compelled to say that Italian coalition politics has changed more cosmetically than in substance. Craxi's record-breaking government of 1983-86 may, however, appear to challenge some of these continuities.

If anything, forming new governments — let alone maintaining them in existence — has become more difficult since the breakdown of the Centre-Left formula in the early 1970s. Because of the greater problems of constructing workable majorities, Italy has from that time experimented with a variety of minority governments, embarked on the three-year long effort at 'National Solidarity' governments involving informal support from the Communist Party (PCI) and then from 1980 turned to the *pentapartito* or five-party formula, which has allowed for rotation in the office of Prime Minister between leaders of the DC and those of other parties. The overall post-war pattern of coalition formulas is shown in the following table (with Prime Ministers in brackets):

Coalition Formations in Italy, 1945–87

1945–47	Cross-party governments, including DC, PCI, and PSI (De Gasperi)
1947–57	Centre-Right governments, including DC, PSDI, PLI, and PRI (De Gasperi, Pella, Fanfani, Scelba, Segni)
1957–63	Mainly DC minority governments (Zoli, Fanfani, Segni, Tambroni, Leone)
1963–72	Centre-Left governments (Moro, Leone, Rumor, Colombo)
1972–73	Centre-Right governments (Andreotti)
1973–74	Centre-Left governments (Rumor)
1974–76	Minority governments led by the DC (Moro)
1976–79	'National Solidarity' governments under the DC, with wide party support including especially the PCI (Andreotti)

1979–80   Centre-Right government (Cossiga)
1980–87   Five-party coalitions—*pentapartito* (Forlani, Spadolini, Fanfani, Craxi)
(Parties involved in coalitions, other than the DC and PCI, have been: Socialists (PSI), Social Democrats (PSDI), Republicans (PRI) and Liberals (PLI))

The weaker stability of coalition formulas in the 1970s and 1980s is evident from this table. At a deeper level, it should be noted that during this same period the country's economy has progressively run out of control with the problems of the balance of payments becoming structural, a very high level of inflation and a chronic public sector deficit. While the scope for governmental action has undoubtedly narrowed, looking at Italy's positon in the international economic environment, the question has also to be asked how much institutional weaknesses (the limited constitutional powers of the executive, the dispersal of decision-making and of course the brevity and incohesion of coalition governments) have themselves contributed to this parlous state of Italy in the 1980s. In other words, we are talking about the persistent problem of the country's 'governability' and more broadly the 'Italian crisis'. This is the basic reason for the issue of institutional reform in recent years.

Whatever differences of opinion there might be about the exact causes of Italy's problem of 'governability', coalition politics must indisputably be at the centre of this problem, so that any investigation of this should throw light on how the country is governed. The picture of arcane procedures described above would suggest that Italian politicians in office, from prime ministers downwards, spend at least as much if not more time on the function of coalition management and internal party manoeuvres than on the task of policy-making as such, inferring that the latter must surely suffer. This is the impression conveyed to the public, for as the editor of one of the major quality newspapers has commented: 'The intentions of the political elites are hardly very perceptible to the ordinary members of the public'; then, referring to the formation of the Craxi government in the summer of 1983,

> ... these are therefore the moves of the parties that at this moment are interweaving in the different corridors of power; but for the country at large all this matters very little, even though it appreciates the novelty of a possible Socialist Prime Minister as an event without precedent in the history of Italy.[2]

Yet, what is the real situation looked at, so to speak, from inside the institutions, if that is possible? Does in reality coalition politics accord with the image which (as noted) is very negative?

One serious problem in assessing this subject is the lack of hard evidence. Compared with many countries, politicians in Italy have been noticeably reticent in recording their experiences of government, perhaps understandably because it is usually premature to speak of their 'retiring' from the game of politics, and also because of the corrupt underbelly of the Italian political world. Nobody, it would seem, has been free from being tainted from having held office, so that revelations about others might only rebound against indiscreet memoir-writers. The important period of 'National Solidarity' with Communist involvement in government decisions (1976–79) did produce various accounts by leading politicians, but these were somewhat stylised and certainly to the acute observer of everyday politics they revealed essentially little.[3] The press naturally covers the blow-by-blow process of coalition politics in detail, though whether also in depth is very open to question. The interpretation presented by Italian journalists generally confirms the assumption that competent policy-making is distinctly secondary to office-holding.

There has also been a shortage of academic studies on the subject of Italian coalitions, presumably because of the absence of evidence and because of its inherent complexity. Any general study is so far lacking, but some insights on particular aspects are available. In an essay noting the very absence of systematic work on this question, Pasquino looked at the role of elections in influencing government formations in Italy's multi-party system, taking the 1976 election as an example, and pointed out that the electorate is rarely asked to pronounce clearly on coalition formulas. He concluded that in Italy's case the emphasis has been placed on forming a large consensus around governments rather than on promoting innovating leadership.[4] The absence of alternation in power — essentially because of the PCI's so far limited legitimacy — has tended to stimulate some interest, especially from the mid-1970's with that party's rise in voting support. Again, Giuseppe Di Palma's work on the Italian Parliament drew attention to the growth of legislative concurrence between government and opposition.[6] There has also been scant examination of Italian coalitions on even a descriptive or historical level,[5] let alone explanatory or analytical studies.

The main problem on the interpretive plane is that this subject has suffered too much from one-dimensionality. In some respects, the quotation at the beginning reveals a picture that could be applied to many other West European countries where coalition politics is the norm. For it should be recognised that coalition politics is intrinsically complex, although conceivably the Italian version is more so than elsewhere. The key difficulty is therefore not only finding out 'what actually happened' behind the scenes, but rather establishing the right analytical perspective. In any case, an approach to this subject must be multi-dimensional, for any explanation of Italian coalitional behaviour revolves around the role of the political parties in the full sense, as socio-political as well as institutional forces. In short, the answer lies in Italy's *partitocrazia* ('party state' or literally 'party-ocracy' or 'party power'), i.e. the dominant role of parties in the operation of the system and the considerable extent to which partisan allegiance permeates public life.

The one-dimensionality noted above comes from focusing solely or too exclusively on the institutional dimension of Italian coalition politics. This follows the path of conventional coalition studies, whether theoretical or empirical, which have usually concentrated on the institution of the cabinet as the assumed centre of decision-making with its composition and policy agreements being the main criteria for estimating the dividends acquired by individual coalition partners. This line of enquiry is significant in reflecting on the relative weight of the different parties in government at any one moment, but it can only be one side of the story. That is particularly so on Italy, where as a consequence of institutional weaknesses policy-making is hardly concentrated exclusively within the cabinet and more often than not key influences over it are located outside that institution. Major political figures have sometimes been at the head of Italy's government, (e.g. De Gasperi, Fanfani, Moro and Andreotti), but the office of Prime Minister as such is severely circumscribed, certainly when compared with the same position in other Western European democracies. In general, with the exception of De Gasperi in the immediate post-war period, the Italian Prime Ministership (or Presidency of the Council, as it is officially called) has provided mediative rather than innovative leadership within the framework of multi-party coalitions.[7]

As a rule, the most influential operators in Italian coalition politics are the parties' general secretaries, who invariably are not members of the cabinet. This is what Antonio Ghirelli, former head of President Pertini's press office, meant when he wrote that, while Pertini sought to reinforce parliamentary prerogatives as in accepting prime-ministerial resignations only after a no-confidence motion: 'but naturally all of us take account of the fact that the substance of political conflict lies elsewhere.'[8] With the DC, it is the faction leaders or usually several of them acting in concert who are the party's wire-pullers. That party's Political Secretary usually is a key individual figure in coalition crises, though not literally always. It is significant, for example, that the linchpin in the DC during the 'National Solidarity' *rapprochement* with the PCI was Aldo Moro (whose formal position was President of the DC National Council rather than Political Secretary), and that he deliberately declined to serve in the cabinet, even as Prime Minister, because he would be more influential outside it. According to Andreotti, who assumed the role of Prime Minister, in his diary:

> I extended the invitation once more to Moro that he should preside over the government, disposed as I was to stay outside or within it as he saw fit. He rejects this firmly. He thinks he can help from outside perhaps in an irreplaceable way, given that in the DC's parliamentary group he has woven a relationship with persons that places a premium on manoeuvres and factions. Also with the other parties he thinks he can be useful without a direct personal responsibility.[9].

The conclusion that emerges so far is that a vital distinction has to be drawn between formal structures and 'real' government, and that with the latter informal processes count for more than formal procedures. Hence, looking at coalition politics 'from inside the institutions' as previously suggested will by no means provide the essential story.

Certainly, the political parties as the ultimate source of power 'populate' the various institutions, including the bureaucracy and the media, but they are so omnipresent that any judgement on their overall role has to consider a whole variety of other dimensions. These may be listed as follows: the evolution, articulation and implementation of party strategies, the incidence of party ideologies, the relevance of internal party structural and participatory features, the pull of the parties' electoral audiences, constraints and pressures on leaders from activists and members as well as possibilities or mechanisms whereby leaders may seek to carry their followers (both activist and electoral) along their strategic paths, the actual importance for individual parties of their programmes, traditions of cooperation or not with other political parties, the question of personal-political harmony between top leaders of different parties in forming and maintaining coalitions, and the relationship between social structure and the party system in the sense of how particular parties cooperating at the governmental level might be constrained by the social cleavages they represent. In other words, there is a multiplicity of factors—attitudinal, structural and behavioural — which have to be taken into account when evaluating motivation in Italian coalition politics.

This multi-dimensional approach applied to Italy's *partitocrazia* suggests indeed that governing that country is a complicated and elaborate business, and in this sense there is truth in the popular image of the Italian government described at the beginning of this article.

However, examining this multi-dimensional approach yields further insights into the subject, and in fact points to continuities in coalition politics. While there is no space here to explore all the factors mentioned above or in detail,[10] some common leitmotivs will briefly be drawn out.

Firstly, party strategies feature prominently and continuously in political debate in Italy. One thinks obviously of the PCI's 'historic compromise', the DC's response with *confronto* or 'entente', the PSI's previous pursuit of the 'Left alternative' and now the PCI's 'Democratic alternative'. However, it is vital to abandon the notion that political parties are simple units or somehow cohesive entities in the game of coalition politics, despite the pull of party loyalties. This is particularly essential to stress when looking at the Italian case because of the importance of internal factions or *correnti* in the operation of the parties, especially those with long service in government. This leads us to considering the relationship between inter and intra-party behaviour, and also to vertical relations within party structures and how these impinge on party strategies in practice. This approach may seem to be another way of saying that political parties are 'coalitions within themselves', yet this obvious point needs a sharper focus when discussing government coalitions.[11] Hence, it follows that political elites may be far from free agents for they are usually subject to a variety of pressures, often contradictory, and some more visible to outsiders than others.

Secondly, it is misleading to consider parties as merely institutional forces without reference to their socio-political roles. Party leaders might appear to the public to be guilty of *verticismo* (elitism or 'summitry' in a pejorative sense), and there is of course a certain confidentiality about inter-party negotiations. But, nevertheless, the social bases of the parties cannot be ignored, not least because they are the channels for the expression of interests, the representatives of particular constituencies and the carriers of ideologies. One Communist member of parliament explained this lucidly:

> You keep talking about parliamentarians and the electorate as if they were some sort of undifferentiated and disembodied entities floating in mid-air. But behind them is a definite reality, which is made up of parties, organisations, ideologies, historical commitments, and divisions, which is the Italian reality. I don't know any such thing as the electorate in general. I know there are electorates of each party, each with its own...demands and aspirations, and this is the reality which we recognise... You ask each member of parliament about his ideas, what he does...but these questions don't have any sense if you ignore the parties and the social classes to which we belong...It's understood that each member of parliament feels that he

has particular responsibilities towards his base and his party, because after all we are a country with strong party organisations.[12]

Clearly, there is much scope for party variation on this point. It would be expected that a Communist leader would speak more emphatically in such terms than either a Socialist or a Christian Democrat, and particularly more so than a leader of one of the small parties which lack the mass base and organisational articulation of the major parties. So far as the need for social consensus determines coalitional behaviour, therefore, a distinction has necessarily to be drawn between the major parties and the small ones.

Electoral pressures or movements are bound to promote or constrain coalitional options, although it is not easy to disentangle influence from rationalisation. It is interesting to observe how party elites actually interpret or instrumentalise election trends. Invariably, the different parties make a habit of reading their own strategic preferences into election results, and they predictably use voting success as a bargaining counter in subsequent coalition talks. For instance a significant electoral advance was crucial to Craxi's strategy as PSI leader in furthering his party's role in government and in becoming Prime Minister. The June 1983 election produced only a modest advance for the Socialists beyond the roughly 10 per cent of previous elections, but what opened the way or his elevation to the Palazzo Chigi was the unprecedented fall in DC support, undercutting that party's previous obstruction of Craxi's aim (as had been only too evident during his first attempt to form a government in 1979). This electoral factor may also work in a negative direction. The PCI's support for the Andreotti governments in the late 1970s was considerably weakened by growing restlessness among party activists over the absence of expected policy results, trade union militancy over economic sacrifices and, not least, electoral setbacks for the PCI, beginning with local elections in 1978. As Ghirelli noted from his vantage point in the presidential palace, Berlinguer was becoming convinced 'that only moving back into opposition could stem an electoral downfall of the party'.[13]

Thirdly, discussion of Italian coalition politics cannot pass without mention of the sub-national level.[14] Italy is still a largely centralised State, although from 1970 government was cautiously devolved to regional structures across the country, not to mention the existence of 94 provinces and over 8,000 communes (some of which have national visibility, like the large cities of Rome, Naples, Milan, Turin and Florence). Coalitional behaviour at this level has always provided some pointer to how party strategies looked in practice, and this possibility was bound to increase with the introduction of the 'ordinary' regions in the 1970s. Parties have felt rather freer to 'experiment' with new options in local politics, most notably in the DC's case with the 'opening to the Left' in the early 1960s and its formation of coalitions with the PSI first of all in certain northern cities. Also, more recently, non-Left parties have been less reluctant to agree to alliances with the PCI sub-nationally; and, indeed, if the latter has performed a governmental role in Italy it has been in several regions and most major cities, especially after its rise in electoral support in the mid-1970s. Certainly, alliances in regional and local politics enter the calculations of party leaders, both generally as part of their overall strategies and also specifically as a point of argument in the formation and maintenance of national coalitions.

In other words, centre-periphery relations form an interesting dimension of some consequence in the functioning of Italy's *partitocrazia*. They furthermore raise in a different form the question of elite control over alliance behaviour at lower levels of the State structure, or vice versa, how far vertical constraints from below operate on national leaders. As a rule, the structural mechanisms of control by the elites are strong, although this is more pronounced with the parties which have strong organisations, above all the PCI. Nevertheless, party leaders lower down possess some autonomy, and this might have some influence on national choices. It is more evident in the case of the PSI and especially the small parties, because they tend to depend on the major parties for alliance possibilities, in regional and local as well as national politics. More generally, the variation in party strengths across the country, the different ideological colouration of the parties in different localities (notably with respect to the DC's various *correnti*), not to mention indigenous problems facing different city governments all condition the scope for and implementation of coalitions at that level.

Fourthly, it should be no surprise to those aware of Italy as a 'penetrated system' that international constraints enter into that country's coalition politics. This has usually taken the form of American pressure on the Christian Democrats against any opening towards the Communists, an influence based on considerations of ideology and defence strategy. Keeping Washington happy has long been a routine in the formulation of new coalitions in Italy, as seen in President Kennedy's lifting of the USA's veto on the Centre-Left alliance with the Socialists and the visits there of DC politicians but also Socialist leaders (such as Craxi in the years before his eventual takeover as the first Socialist Prime Minister) at key stages in changes in coalition formations. Italian politicians can, however, be starkly cynical about this side of coalition formations. Following the 1976 election, which saw a dramatic rise in

Communist voting support, not only the Americans but also some
European heads of government exerted pressure on Rome, sometimes
crudely. Andreotti wrote in his diary in July 1976, after Chancellor
Schmidt's blunt statement that Italy would become isolated if the PCI
came to power:

> I believe that we must not show ourselves hysterical or touchy. We will
> have time to explain to the Chancellor the situation and ask his advice. He
> represents the country to which we have had to pledge gold from the
> monetary reserve to guarantee the latest loans. We cannot feel offended
> because he busies himself with what happens with us . . . us debtors. I
> firmly oppose any public polemics with Bonn on this matter . . . I find
> myself between the hammer and the anvil: I cannot deny that to a large
> degree the protest is right (the public controversy over Schmidt's statement),
> but it would be serious for Italian interests to engage in controversy with the
> Chancellor of Federal Germany. The agreement between the political
> parties is essential, but so too must we be in agreement with partner and
> allied countries. I continue the complicated action of fireman . . .[15]

The real influence of such international opinion on Italian domestic
politics might be declining, both with the PCI's increasing legitimacy
(and greater distance from Moscow since its direct attack on Soviet
policy after the scotching of the Polish experiment of 1980–81) and the
precedent set by Communist parties in government elsewhere in Western
Europe. Nevertheless, international constraints have in the past been
present in the way in which changes in coalition formulas with the
political Left moving into the 'area of government' — first the PSI in the
1960s, then the PCI in the 1970s — were accompanied by the party in
question modifying its stand on major foreign issues, such as membership
of the European Community and of NATO, among other things to
accommodate foreign opinion.

Fifthly, and finally, Italian politics is noted for the informality and
subtlety of its alliance relationships. Informal coalitions (i.e. where
partner-parties are not actually present in the cabinet) are not unknown
in other countries, but they have been developed to an extraordinary
extent in the case of Italy. For instance, there may occur 'legislative
coalitions' involving more than *ad hoc* support for government policy
items by the opposition, and these are not necessarily co-terminous with
'executive coalitions', i.e. other parties may give external or parliamentary floor support to those in power. During the 1970s, there was a
greater articulation of informal alliance arrangements once the PCI
emerged as a potential party of government. The 'National Solidarity'
governments of Andreotti during 1976–79 progressed from a state of

non-sfiducia or 'no non-confidence' (the PCI and other parties agreed to abstain from voting in Parliament), through the 'programmatic agreement' of 1977–78 based on a joint policy document between the DC minority government and the PCI, PSI, PSDI, PRI and PLI to the 1978–79 situation, when the DC accepted the PCI as part of the formal parliamentary majority *(nella maggioranza)* and there was a re-negotiated government programme. The point to make about this is that a variety of informal coalition solutions — assisted by the convoluted political language that accompanies alliance relationships — makes for flexibility in managing or containing ideological differences between conveying parties. What this says about the cohesion of Italian coalitions is another matter, let alone the confusion sowed among the country's voters and outside observers of the Italian political scene!

In conclusion, this last feature of Italian politics draws attention to a general lesson of coalitional behaviour. An important distinction should be made between what may be called the arithmetical and political dimensions, the former being simply the total of parliamentary seats enjoyed by the different parties (conventional coalition studies have concentrated particularly on this aspect, though sometimes too exclusively so). What may be arithmetically possible is not necessarily politically feasible; equally, what may be politically desirable — on the part of intending coalition partners — may not be arithmetically possible, For example, Berlinguer and other PCI leaders argued after the 1983 election that the 'numerical conditions' now existed for a 'democratic majority' without the DC,[16] but this proved politically a non-starter because the DC and PSI, albeit with their different motives, were set on a reproduction of the *pentapartito* formula. What is interesting in practice is the actual relationship or interaction between the arithmetical and political dimensions, for the distinction between the two can rarely be a clear-cut one. Election results create arithmetical possibilities in the game of coalition options, but they may be said to pronounce on the credibility of coalition alternatives, depending on the extent to which party leaders have made prior commitments and these are 'debated' in the election campaign.

A closer examination of Italy's coalition politics from a multi-dimensional standpoint based on that country's pervasive *partitocrazia* does therefore reveal elements of continuity. It also becomes clearer that coalition politics is by nature a complicated business, and that as such Italy is not necessarily so vastly different from other countries. The picture conveyed here of a multiplicity of interlocking and conflicting factors which lie behind the surface impression of confusion in the practice of Italian govenment does naturally put the first Socialist Prime

Ministership into a more sober perspective than Craxi's performance might suggest, however much it might be of historical significance. While the PSI has benefited from the DC's recent weaknesses, it has yet to consolidate its new 'centrality'—at least electorally.

Overall, therefore, any understanding of Italian coalitions has to proceed from an examination of what happens inside the political parties rather than inside the institutions. While not departing from the common view about Italy's weak government, looking closely at coalitions there does help to explain the behaviour of that country's political elites.

NOTES

Some of the ideas in this chapter are drawn from the author's 'Party Politics and Coalition Government in Italy' in Vernon Bogdanor (ed.), *Coalition in Western Europe*, Heinemann, London, 1983, pp. 200-230.

1   George Armstrong in *The Guardian*, 26 January 1972.
2   *La Repubblica*, 22 July 1983.
3   These included Giulio Andreotti, *Diari 1976-79* Rizzoli, Milano, 1981; Andrea Manzella, *Il Tentativo La Malfa*, Il Mulino, Bologna, 1980; Giovanni Spadolini, *Da Moro a La Malfa*, Vallecchi, Firenze, 1979; F. Di Giulio and E. Rocco, *Il Ministro-Ombra si confessa*, Rizzoli, Milano, 1979.
4   G. Pasquino, 'Per un'analisi delle coalizioni di governo in Italia' in A. Parisi and G. Pasquino, *Continuità e Mutamento Elettorale in Italia*, Il Mulino, Milano, 1977.
5   G. Di Palma, *Surviving without Governing: the Italian parties in Parliament*, Univ. of California Press, Berkeley, 1977.
6   eg see A. Marradi, 'Italy: from "Centrism" to Crisis of the Centre-Left Coalitions' in E. Browne & J. Dreijmanis (ed), *Government Coalitions in Western Democracies*, Longman, New York, 1982.
7   See S. Cassese, 'Is there a Government in Italy? Politics and Administration at the Top' in R. Rose and E. Suleiman (ed), *Presidents and Prime Ministers*, American Enterprise Institute, Washington D.C., 1980.
8   Antonio Ghirelli, *Caro Presidente*, Rizzoli, Milano, 1981, p. 80.
9   Andreotti, op. cit., p 189, entry for 6 March 1978.
10 For further discussion, see Geoffrey Pridham, 'Party Politics and Coalition Government in Italy', in Vernon Bogdanor (ed), *Coalition Government in Western Europe*, Heinemann, London, 1983, pp. 200-230. Also the author's forthcoming book, *Political Parties and Coalitional Behaviour in Italy*, Croom Helm, London, 1987.
11 Some attention has been paid to party factions of the DC in coalition politics, see A. Zuckerman, *The Politics of Faction: Christian Democratic Rule in Italy*, Yale UP, New Haven, 1979.
12 Quoted in Di Palma, op. cit., pp. 160-61.
13 Ghirelli, op. cit., p 80.
14 On this, see Geoffrey Pridham, 'Parties and Coalition Behaviour in Italian Local Politics: conflict or convergence?' in *European Journal of Political Research*, September 1984, pp. 223-41.
15 Andreotti, op. cit., pp. 20-1 and 23, entries for 13 July and 17 July 1976.
16 *La Stampa*, 28 giugno 1983.

HUNTING THE VOTE
BUILDING ELECTORAL CONSENSUS
IN CALABRIA

James Walston

THERE is a presumption on the part of journalists, scholars and the political actors themselves that public life in the South of Italy is regulated almost entirely by clientelistic methods. A picture is painted of the South in which political support and the bureaucratic machine function on the basis of personal relationships; public resources are distributed as a personal favour of those in power (elected or nominated politician or bureaucrat) rather than as the right of the citizen or local administration. Private or party gain is taken as the motivation in public behaviour, with the vote or public resources (finance, housing, health, bureaucratic permits and so on) as the currency.

In this article I shall try to determine how far this picture corresponds to reality in the region of Calabria in the post-war period. The political system will be described in general terms, drawing attention both to its fixed points and its mutations over the last forty years. In the second section there will be two case studies of individual politicians to illustrate the system in practice. I will conclude by comparing the two examples with the type of politician at present in control of the region and will suggest the ways in which public life and politicians have changed over the years and the ways in which they have remained the same.

THE SYSTEM

1. Electoral Competition

We will start with the truism that different electoral systems produce different forms of electoral competition. The peculiarities and mechanics of each individual system have very clear effects on the way political campaigns are waged. This is not to put forward a purely determinstic view of political culture; I am not suggesting that the mechanics of a system govern the whole of political behaviour, but the effects are there and cannot be ignored.[1]

Italian proportional representation is based on large constituencies which usually cover two or more provinces and may return up to fifty-three deputies. The voter gives support to a party and then has the option of giving up to four preference votes to individual candidates. Once the number of seats a party has won has been established, it is the preference votes that decide which of the party's candidates have become deputies. This means that, in common with other systems, there is pre-electoral competition within each party in order to establish which candidates should stand. But in contrast with most other systems, there is considerable competition during the election campaign. Whereas in most other proportional representation systems, the order in which candidates will be elected is decided by the party prior to the election campaign, in Italy it is the preference vote which decides who will go to Parliament. The arena is outside the party, among the electors, a circumstance which in the southern Italian case encourages clientelistic practices. The competition takes place at five different levels: (*a*) interparty rivalry; (*b*) interprovince rivalry; (*c*) interfactional rivalry; (*d*) interlobby rivalry (*e*) interpersonal rivalry.

Thus voters may simply vote the party and not use their preference vote. Or they may vote between one and four individuals as well. In the second case, having chosen the party, they may choose the local candidate, for example from Cosenza rather than Reggio; one faction rather than another, for example Forze Nuove rather than the Fanfaniani; candidates endorsed by one lobby rather than another, such as the Coltivatori Diretti rather than the CISL, and finally one individual rather than another—Bianchi instead of Rossi. In practice, of course, the choice is neither as articulate as this, nor is it made in this order.[2]

There are unfortunately no in-depth studies over a period of time of the Italian voter in the same way as there have been in the United States, the United Kingdom and Sweden, so it is not possible to establish with any precision why voters have changed or maintained their party or individual loyalty at the national level, let alone for the constituency of Calabria. We must therefore fall back on more general interpretations of voting shifts.

If we consider the changing strengths of the various parties in Calabria since 1946, there are a number of observations which can be made in order to interpret these changes.

TABLE 1

ELECTORAL RESULTS, CHAMBER OF DEPUTIES, CALABRIA (%)

Source: ISTAT

Date	PCI	PSI	PSDI	PRI	DC	PLI	PNM	PMP	MSI	Other
1946	12.1	11.1a	2.4b	4.1	34.3	11.0c			7.9d	12.8e
1948	(29.5f)		2.1g	3.2	48.8	8.1c	1.5		5.4	1.0
1953	20.9	11.2	2.7	2.1	40.6	3.5	8.8		7.7	
1958	23.0	13.2	1.9	0.6	47.4	2.7	2.0	3.2	5.8	
1963	25.2	12.5	2.9	1.3	42.2	3.4	1.7h		6.6	
1968	22.8	(17.1i)		2.3	40.1	2.5	0.6h		5.2	4.2a
1972	28.6	10.3	2.7	2.0	41.3	1.7			9.7	3.5j
1976	32.9	11.5	2.7	2.1	39.4	0.7			8.8	2.0k
1979	26.7	12.8	3.2	1.7	42.7	0.7			7.0	5.2l
1983	26.2	16.1	4.9	3.6	36.8	0.9			7.7	3.8

a PSIUP
b Partito d'Azione
c Blocco nazionale delle libertà
d Uomo Qualunque
e Unione democratica nazionale
f FDP
g Unità socialista
h PDIUM
i PSU
j PSIUP 1.9%, PC(ML) lt 0.3%, Manifesto 0.7%, Mov. Pop. Lav. 0.6%
k DP 1.5%, PR 0.5%
l DN-CD 0.5%, PDUP 1.8%, PR 1.(%,NSU 0.8%, Part. Pop. Cal 0.2%

The high Christian Democrat poll in 1948 can be explained by the immense amount of Cold War propaganda which was used by the party, and which was extremely successful in persuading voters throughout the country that any vote not for the DC was tantamount to inviting Stalin to take over Italy.

The slump which followed was the direct effect of disaffection on the part of Southern notables and was reflected all over the South. The landowning middle and upper classes were unhappy with the agrarian reforms and other populist measures which were taken as a form of creeping socialism. Self-styled 'independent' fortnightlies of the period (*Battaglia Calabra* and *Corriere delle Calabrie*) gave limited support to monarchists and neo-Fascists as well as to the DC; from 1953 onwards, they were solidly behind the DC.

In a sense, of course, this is proof of clientelism in action since the notables were able to shift large numbers of votes from the DC to the right-wing parties. However, it is of a different order to the type of clientelism which followed, as we shall see. The patron-client relationship in this case was not a political one but an economic one; the agricultural labourer voted for the employer's man not because he himself had any relationship with the politician, nor because he thought he would derive any gain from the politician's election, but because his boss would.

By 1958 the election results show how the DC's takeover of the State and public bodies at a local level was paying off in electoral terms. For the most part, however, Calabrian voting patterns follow the national ones, with a fairly constant difference maintained between the Calabrian and the national figures. Two results, though, are clearly anomalous; the PSU in 1968 and the Neo-Fascists in 1972.

The first result was due to the energy and achievements of one man, Giacomo Mancini. He was the second Calabrian cabinet minister since 1948, and in contrast to the other minister, Gennaro Cassiani, was seen to have introduced considerable progress and to have brought many benefits to the region. As Minister for Public Works he was responsible for doubling the single track railway on the Tyrrhenian coast and building the Salerno-Reggio motorway, as well as a large number of lesser projects. Most of these had been planned long before the Centre-Left governments which brought Mancini to the ministry, but he was credited (and to a large extent correctly) with actually starting these projects. Apart from the benefits of Mancini's sojourn in the Ministry of Public Works, the campaign itself was exceptional in that it was particularly aggressive ('American' is the adjective most commonly used) and made wide use of all that the media could offer in Calabria in the late Sixties.

The Fascist gains in the following elections were largely limited to the province of Reggio, and most of them were in the city. They were directly related to the riots of 1970, when the city exploded on learning that Catanzaro would be the regional capital. Popular discontent was ably expoited by the Right and the 1972 results were the fruit. Subsequent results show the protest vote for what it was as percentages return to something close to their previous levels.

This brief overview of Calabrian electoral behaviour illustrates that by no means all political change can be attributed to clientelist methods. We should now examine the areas where clientelism is effective. Given the state of the region over the whole period under examination, control of credit is perhaps the single most important element in the construction of political power.

2. The Banks

The most important source of credit in Calabria is the regional savings bank, the *Cassa di Risparmio della Calabria* (after 1956, *della Calabria e della Lucania*). Like all savings banks in Italy, the *Cassa di Risparmio* is not a State agency but is strictly controlled by the law and is used in order to distribute State funds. Members of the board are political appointees while the employees are in theory not allowed to hold political posts. From the beginning, however, there has been a clear link between the *Cassa* and the local parties or factions of them.

The bank has its head offices in Cosenza, which explains the pre-eminence of that city over the other two in political terms, at least until other centres of power were built up in Reggio and Catanzaro (most obviously in regional government, whose assembly sits in Reggio and executive in Catanzaro).

The first clear intimation of bank involvement in politics came when the President, Luigi De Matera, was replaced by his vice-president, Alfio Pisani, in February 1953 (before his mandate was up). The Pisani family were large landowners in the nothern part of the province of Cosenza. They had not been affected by the land reforms and remained faithful to the DC, albeit always on the right of the party. Alfio's brother, Baldo, was for a long time President of the provincial government and one of the provincial leaders of the DC. The Communist senator, Francesco Spezzano, complained in Parliament that the change in the presidency had taken place just a few months before a general election and that the new President was a person too closely linked to a political figure.[3] The careers of the bank's senior management and their relations show how important the institute was in the province's political life.

There are also episodes directly linked with the election of certain individuals (always within the DC, but the bank played and plays an important role in the infraparty competition). The best documented case is that of Dario Antoniozzi's success as a candidate in the 1953 general election, described by Spezzano. As the Communist Senator pointed out:

> The candidate Dario Antoniozzi, a young man about 25–26 years old [actually 29, he was born in 1923], a first time candidate, was the second candidate elected in the Christian Democrat list with 62,430 preference votes. The obscure and unknown young man comes in ahead of two Junior Ministers . . . He beats one of them—and I emphasise this point—by 20,000 votes or about 33%, and the second by 12,000 or about 21%. He came in before six sitting deputies among whom there are names which carry a certain weight and reputation . . .[4]

His father was Director General of the *Cassa di Risparmio*.

In 1958, just before the elections, an opposition paper claimed that new employees were being hired without going through the competitive examinations (*concorsi*) as laid down both by the bank's statute and a decree of the board.[5] This is a frequent ploy used to gain electoral support. It was used in the same year in Reggio Calabria, where there was a prefectorial commissioner who gave jobs to some 300 people in the local administration. Once again the move was to the advantage of the DC.

Nor did the bank operate in isolation; there were links between it and other sources of influence. One of the 'independent' papers mentioned, *Corriere delle Calabrie*, functioned as the mouthpiece of senior management, with every issue full of their speeches and those of their political protegés. Advertising in the paper was almost monopolised by the bank and was a large source of income.

In the same paper, one can see signs of the link with another important source of political power in the Fifties: the Church. Each new branch was blessed either by the parish priest or the local bishop and the paper printed photos of the ecclesiastic in the company of Alfio Pisani, the president, and Florindo Antoniozzi, the director general.

Although it is a tendency which can be seen to have decreased in the Seventies and Eighties, blood and artificial kinship are still important features in tying together control of votes, public bodies and the economy. The son of the director general was Dario Antoniozzi. The deputy director of the bank at the time, Salvatore Perugini, was the councillor in charge of finances in the comune of Cosenza (*assessore comunale alle finanze*). Previously, Perugini had been president of the city council housing agency (IACP, Istituto Autonomo Case Popolari), an important part of the structure of political power which we will consider under a separate heading. In 1958, the provincial secretary of the DC, Mario Cristofaro, resigned in order to become a candidate at the general election. Perugini was nominated secretary in his place but was forced to resign soon afterwards because of the incompatibility with his post at the bank. His son-in-law was elected secretary in his place.

Perugini's son, Pasquale, was elected a member of the Christian Democrat Provincial Committee in 1956 and the following year became a member of the board (*consiglio d'amministrazione*) of the Sila Reform Agency (OVS, Opera Valorizzazione Sila). His career through the provincial and regional governments has relied heavily on the support of the OVS. After he retired from the presidency of the regional government, he became president of the OVS which became an agricultural development agency in 1965, ESAC (Ente Sviluppo Agricolo Calabria).

The web is clearly described by the Communist fortnightly *Risveglio Cosentino*.[6] The DC leader in Calabria, Gennaro Cassiani, was married to a Stancati (one of the directors of the bank), Florindo Antoniozzi was married to a Cassiani, a brother-in-law of Cassiniani's was married to a sister of Antoniozzi's. Another brother-in-law was a director of the parastate health insurance agency, INAM, while another relative was secretary of the Cosenza City Council. As we have already mentioned, Alfio Pisani's brother, Baldo, was president of the provincial administration. Baldo was also president of the Cosenza Automobile Club (ACI) a quasi-public entity in that it is one of the agencies entitled to collect road tax and issue the tax disc, and the infant and maternity welfare agency (ONMI, Opera Nazionale Maternità Infanzia). The son-in-law of the bank's deputy director general was a provincial councillor; an uncle was a city councillor. Four other city councillors were part of the deputy director general's group.

This type of structure continues over time; Dario Antoniozzi's brother-in-law, Giorgio Stancati, was a director of the BNL (Banca Nazionale del Lavoro).[7]

More recently another relation of Antoniozzi, Mario Laganà, became a director (*consigliere*) of the Bank of Naples and the State funding bank, Isveimer. From 1979 to 1983 he, too, was a deputy.

Even in the Seventies with the growth of other sources of credit, the *Cassa di Risparmio* controlled one third of the savings in the region.[8]

With the growth of the Centre-Left and of Mancini's power in the Sixties, some of the control of the bank went to the PSI. For most of the Seventies, a Manciniano was President. The more blatant electioneering went but the Institute still commanded considerable power which could be used for party or personal advancement.

Although Cosenza remains the seat of the bank's main office, the growth of the regional government in the 1970s and 1980s meant that provincial differences have become less accentuated. So much so that mafia influences reached the bank although direct mafia influence was limited to the province of Reggio (see below, section 4). In 1986 the Bank of Italy pointed out that the *Cassa di Risparmio* had lent funds to individuals involved with mafia. A subsequent Parliamentary Anti-mafia Commission report maintained that loans had not been made directly to mafiosi but that the bank had been granting credit on personal grounds rather than on creditworthiness.[9] It was later admitted that the bank had lit.540 bn. of bad debts out of loans totalling lit.3,000 bn. In March 1987, the Bank of Italy appointed commissioners and temporarily dismissed the board of directors. The commissioners had the task of introducing order into the running of the bank and bringing it back into financial health. In practice this meant calling in many of the loans which had been granted for political rather than financial reasons. At the same time, a magistrate from Locri in the province of Reggio Calabria ordered the arrest of a number of members of the board. They were accused of granting some lit.50 bn. of credit to a local citrus processing plant whose credit was already grossly overextended.[10]

Over the post-war period, therefore, the local savings bank has had considerable weight in building political support and vote-winning. In the Fifties this influence was more visible because control over the institution was concentrated in the hands of a few families and in one party. Since then the DC has become factionalised and the PSI has been introduced into the equation; so power is more dispersed. The bank is therefore all the more significant since it is not only a means of winning votes but also an arena in itself.

3. IACP (Istituto Autonomo, Case Popolari) and USL (Unità di Sanità Locale)

Various articles in Mario Caciagli's account of Catania in the 1970s[11] point out how public agencies are used to build up electoral support. He and his collaborators consider among others the municipal transport company, the hospital and the public housing agency. Here we will consider the housing agencies and the public health boards in the Calabrian context. As the name suggests, the IACP are independent agencies on a provincial basis whose task is to provide low cost housing in a similar way to council housing in the UK while the USL are the management committees set up under the health service reforms in order to coordinate all aspects of health care in a given area. Naturally both bodies are appointed on a party basis following the parties' relative strengths in the given area.

Already in the Fifties there were episodes which showed how the Institute in Cosenza was being used for electoral and party gain. As part of the spoils system (*lottizzazione*) which was and is an integral part of ruling coalitions at the local and national level, the presidency of the Cosenza IACP went to a Social Democrat Florindo De Luca. De Luca was promptly accused by the Christian Democrat paper *Battaglia Calabra* of accepting the job 'in order to create a great deal of sympathy for his party' so that at the next election Cosenza would send a lot of Social Democrats to Parliament'.[12] The remark is not only an inference on De Luca's probity and an attack on the PSDI but is a reflection of the writer's view of the purpose of public agencies. Indeed two years later De Luca was ousted in order to give the DC complete control.[13]

As the Socialist Party became part of both national and local government in the Sixties so it gradually took up positions of responsibility in public agencies. In 1983, the board in Cosenza had three Christian Democrats, two Communists and three Socialists, despite the fact that the PSI takes only about twenty per cent of the poll in the province. But given the determining weight of the PSI in coalition building, the party was over-represented in all such bodies. The same feature can be noticed in the USL (Unità Sanità Locale, the health service management committees) and throughout the country where the PSI polls much less than twenty per cent. In Cosenza there is a similar overlap of jobs on public bodies, political posts and family links. The Socialist mayor of Cosenza in the 1980s was an employee of the IACP before becoming mayor. He then went on to become a member of the Regional government. One brother was the UIL representative for hospital workers and a member of the IACP board while another brother was on the board of the *Cassa di Risparmio*. His father-in-law was the Provincial Secretary of the UIL.

The power of the IACP as a political machine covers a wide spectrum. The Institute builds houses and therefore has considerable funds available. These are assigned to certain construction companies rather than others. It has a provincial responsibility to fulfil the need for council housing and therefore has leverage over the single *comuni* in the province. A member of PDUP who had served for seven years on the IACP board (as a PCI nominee) maintained that funds were only given to *comuni* which were 'friendly' to the majority of the board, though he admitted that this was unprovable since all the board's deliberations were strictly legal. The job-giving capacity of the IACP is a third source of power. Finally, there is the assignment of the houses themselves which is done by a separate committee. The rules establishing who has a right to a house are rigorously laid down by law, but the scoring mechanism can be adjusted before houses are actually assigned. This can only be done if the applicant has special information from within the committee.

Beyond these covert uses of the IACP, there are also some more clamorous examples. In Reggio in the early 1980s, the President controlled the Institute more or less alone without consulting the rest of the board: 'he goes around with a rubber stamp, signs minutes and takes decisions without having had a meeting.'[14]

The Reggio USL has also been used overtly as an electoral support-gathering agency with little regard to procedure or the law. By the mid-1980s it was the biggest employer in the city with 2,500 employees and a budget of lit.270 bn. Not only was it giving supply and building contracts to both Sicilian and Calabrian mafiosi,[15] but was giving jobs to electors of the board itself.[16] Other health boards have even worse records; in March 1987 a number of members of the health management board in Locri in the province of Reggio Calabria were arrested for fraud and embezzlement while the Ministry of Health had been investigating it since 1983.[17]

Like the *Cassa di Risparmio*, the IACP are not the only sources of party or individual political power. Instead, taken together, they are emblematic of the type of control which is exercised over public agencies. Instead of serving their declared interests (in these cases providing a banking service or cheap housing), their main aim is to provide electoral and political support for politicians and parties. To this extent, they are similar to the public health boards (USL), the agricultural development agency (ESAC) and the political institutions themselves (comune, province, region).

4. Organised Crime

Mafia has for long been an important influence in all sections of society in Western Sicily and Southern Calabria. The innovation in recent years is the presence of organised crime as a vote collecting factor in other parts of Calabria: mafia in the province of Reggio, and the more limited and less pervasive gangs of extortionists in Cosenza. The first has been denounced from all sides, the second is still a much more hidden phenomenon muttered to the interviewer in a conspiratorial way but still clear enough from election results.

Under the pseudonym of Gino Malito, Mancini accused a Reggio deputy of having mafia support: 'he does not recruit his supporters either from Catholic Action or from among the Daughters of Mary',[18] an elliptical remark but the closest anyone has come to a direct accusation and clear in the context. In 1977, that same man's private secretary gave a false alibi to a mafia boss involved in a shoot-out with the carabinieri.[19]

Electoral data give surer evidence. If one takes that evidence at a local level, the mafia influence is clear. In the town of Gioia Tauro, the site for first a new steelworks and then a power station and epicentre of mafia in the region, the PRI polled from 0.3 per cent (24 votes) to 1.1 per cent (64 votes) between 1948 and 1963. With no change in local organisation nor in regional or local policy, the same party polled 422 votes (6.4 per cent) in 1968. In the following two elections, their share of the poll slumped to 2.8% and 2.2%. The reason for the startling growth and fall in the PRI percentage is found largely in the tenure of the Ministry of Justice by a Republican. This meant that the party was able to obtain favours such as parole, transfer from one gaol to another—favours obviously useful to the Gioia mafiosi—through the Ministry.

There is a second episode concerning the PRI in Gioia. In December 1978, a Communist councillor from the town testified as a character witness in a mafia trial. Given the PCI's consistent and militant anti-mafia stance, the councillor was expelled from the party. In February he became a Republican and in the June 1979 parliamentary elections he stood as a candidate. The PRI polled 766 votes or 8.8 per cent.[20]

While these figures are not obsolute proof, they are certainly a strong suggestion that mafiosi are involved in politics. This is a view shared by the courts. In the committal proceedings of a big mafia trial in the late 1970s, the investigating magistrate observed that 'the relationship between the mafia and certain politicians is easily deduced from the fact that the mafia organisation is a powerful vote-producing machine and these votes require payments which are equally easily deduced'.[21] The cousin of the Reggio boss, Paolo De Stefano, was elected as a Christian Democrat councillor for the city of Reggio in 1980. It was the first time that he had stood and he was without great party experience. He won the second highest number of preference votes after the outgoing mayor and ahead of all the other ex-councillors.

More recently, a senior Reggio Christian Democrat stated that there was an organisation which linked members of his own party with certain Socialists and certain Social Democrats; the chain was supposedly mafia. Certainly links between parts of the three major parties (and the PRI) in the city were apparent for many years previously. In his speech at the beginning of the judicial year in January 1986, the senior magistrate in Calabria calculated that some 15% of the total vote in the province of Reggio was controlled by mafia; this produced 30% of local politicians under direct mafia influence. In 1986 there were 112 murders in the province of Reggio (20.14 per 100,000, a higher rate than either Reggio itself or Palermo in the post-war period). Of these, nine were contractors for the city council.[22]

In Cosenza there is no mafia culture comparable to that of the province of Reggio, but as with most towns in Italy, the protection racket hits all moneymaking enterprises. The combination of the two makes for much more reticence, but my own research suggests that the extortionist gangs also contribute to the vote gathering business. There are two blocks of council houses in Cosenza which were occupied by rival gangs in 1982. Neither have actually been assigned any of the flats but they have not yet been evicted. In the meantime, they reglazed the windows with bullet-proof glass. Beyond the difficulty in police terms of ejecting these unwanted tenants, there was also the fact that the mayor depended for much of his support on criminal elements in the town. One respondent, a local deputy, believed that 'in the Cosenza area the route used is probably direct intimidation with these people being taken on as electoral helpers or bill posters; this becomes support for a certain candidate . . . The [mayor's] group is said to have had this sort of support'.[23] This came from the opposition. Another interviewee, an old Socialist militant, admitted to the author in April 1983 that the mayor of Cosenza did win votes from the criminal gangs. A local sociologist also hinted at the connection but without any direct identification: 'There have been various cases in which a particularly unscrupulous sector of the politcal elite has not resisted the temptation to use the gangsters' power in political and electoral competition.[24] The electoral data confirm this view in that in 1980, before becoming mayor, the figure accused of using the gangster vote won almost double the number of preference votes compared with his nearest rival (4,244 as opposed to 2,264).

But as we have seen in the previous section, the then mayor had support from other sectors of the town and was not so dependent on the criminal vote as, say, the Reggio deputy mentioned above who lost his seat when mafia support was transferred to another candidate.

5. The Church

In the post-war period, the DC relied heavily on the organisational powers of the Church in Calabria as elsewhere. The founder of the party in the region was a priest, Don Luigi Nicoletti. Although much of Nicoletti's authority came from his position as a cleric, his power came from the party.

Nationally, the Church took its lead from the violent anti-Communism of Pope Pius XII; locally the symbiosis between DC and church is shown both visually and in print in newspapers of all colours. I have already mentioned the blessing of new branches of the *Cassa di Risparmio*. Representatives of the Church were present at all public functions. Religious festivals in the summer took precedence over the local Communist or Socialist gatherings (Feste dell'Unità or Avanti). In 1958 there was a clear example of a bishop's direct involvement in the infraparty struggle in the DC. Mario Cristofaro, for many years the DC Provincial Secretary, was due to stand for the senatorial constituency of Rossano. He had no strong backers and the Bishop of Rossano preferred a representative of the landowning Berlingieri family. Cristofaro was forced to stand down and move to the less secure ground of the Chamber of Deputies list. Berlingieri was subsequently elected while Cristofaro failed to win enough preference votes.

An indication of the concern of the Church in politics is given by the announcements in Christian Democrat newspapers before the 1958 election warning Catholics that anyone who voted for Marxist parties could be excommunicated. Throughout the period there were fights in the local party press, on the one side against 'the clericals', and on the other side accusations of anticlericalism. This, though, was a phenomenon hardly limited to Calabria in this period.

Following the tendency started under the papacy of John XXIII, over the last twenty years the Church's direct involvement in politics has decreased. In the 1970–71 riots in Reggio the archbishop, Monsignor Ferro, supported the movement in favour of the city as regional capital. Subsequently he declared himself tired of the DC and encouraged the faithful to vote for the MSI which had successfully exploited the riots.

Over the past decade or so, the Church has kept a much lower profile. The Base deputy Riccardo Misasi still allowed himself to be photographed kneeling at prayer (and the photo was published with only a touch of irony) along with an otherwise positive interview in a Communist weekly.[25]

Church influence may still be important within the DC. The Reggio deputy and one of the champions of the 1970 revolt, Giuseppe Reale, was elected in 1972, but did not make it in 1976 largely because of the withdrawal of Monsignor Ferro's support.[26]

In the parishes and in the villages, the power of the church was if anything stronger. A Catholic historian describes how the parish priest in Catona near Reggio, together with a relation, provided political continuity from 1915 until after the Second World War. The priest was the only organisation in the village: for fishermen, with emigrants, a confraternity; he lobbied for a local bank, a secondary school, a village band and so on. His relation founded the forerunner of the DC, the Italian Popular Party (PPI) in 1919, then became political secretary of the Fascist Party, and after liberation, founded the DC and became mayor.[27]

6. Ministers, Ministries and Deputies

The organs and individuals of central government provide the institutional links between centre and periphery as well as giving elected representatives large possibilities of controlling and distributing resources. This distribution of resources may be used directly to win votes in episodes where there is a clear link between action and payoff, or it may be used to gain a more general consensus or the support of a small group which is electorally unimportant but powerful in other ways.

A glance at the lists of preference votes shows how ministerial positions have an obvious correlation with electoral success; there are exceptions which I will also try to explain. Mancini's maximum came after he had been Minister for Public Works for a number of years and had assured large-scale State intervention in the region. The same is true for the Christian Democrat Riccardo Misasi who was Minister of Education and Antoniozzi who was Minister of Tourism and then for

Fine Arts. Junior ministries are no less important; Christian Democrats and Socialists have made clear gains after holding undersecretaryships.

Although the official morality of public service (and indeed the Constitution explicitly) maintains that deputies and ministers should serve the whole country rather than their own constituency, it is an accepted rule that a deputy who becomes a minister should do the best he can for his electors. This rule is made almost explicit by the distribution of the regional provenance of ministers. Throughout the Republic there has been a nearly exact correlation between the population of a given region and the number of ministers from that region. The red regions are slightly under-represented while the white ones slightly over-represented; Calabria has had a marginally higher proportion of ministers than its population would suggest.[28] There are three villages in the province of Cosenza whose mayors are also or have been deputies: Rende, Altomonte and Rogliano. It is no secret that they are much better off than similar villages in the area.

At the higher level we find Antoniozzi setting up large numbers of cooperatives for the conservation of art treasures using the Youth Employment Scheme (*legge* 285) and Misasi mobilising school janitors to vote for him in the 1972 election, when he won over 120,000 preference votes. His control, though, was not limited to the personal power of the minister: he had 'vast and consolidated links with schools in Calabria because he is an ex-minister and also through Senator Smurra, Undersecretary of Education and the Regional Minister of Education, Nicolò.'[29] This is an example of how a politician can build up a mutually advantageous network. None of the three men mentioned above were in competition; on the contrary, they could exchange the votes they controlled for votes that the others controlled to everyone's profit.

Beyond what the deputy or minister can do on his own account, there is the deputy as a mediator. A member of the Cosenza businessman's association put the question very clearly:

> If you want to set up a factory in say, Roggiano, and you want some of the State subsidies which are available, there are two ways of going about it. Either you take the official road: a project plan must be presented to us. We do a feasibility study, a copy goes to the Regional Association. We then send copies to the Ministry for Industry, the Ministry of Agriculture (because the factory would be built in an agricultural area), the two money ministries (Finance and Budget) and the Ministry for State Participation. When all of these have read, digested and agreed on the report, a new report is prepared for the *Cassa per il Mezzogiorno* which will produce the funding. Usual time scale: five years. Or there is the unofficial path: the putative investor goes to his local deputy and tells him that there are great

possibilities in Roggiano. The deputy pretends to consider the profitability of such a project but really weights the electoral gains to be made. He goes to his *capo-corrente* and says: 'We must have a new source of employment in Roggiano because there is great social unrest'. The *capo-corrente* then uses a proportion of the funds unofficially allotted to his faction from the *Cassa per il Mezzogiorno* in order to finance the factory. Time: five months or less. At no stage is economic feasibility taken into account. Occasionally a project might be profitable, but it is very rare and only by chance.[30]

A senior politician's private secretary confirmed this view of how State funding was distributed, adding that there was another method: 'There are consultancy firms which have contacts within the ministries and will see that the *Cassa per il Mezzogiorno's* bureaucratic delays are minimised. The beneficiary gives the firm five or ten per cent of the funds allotted. This is not part of the contract'.[31]

However, it is not true to say that all deputies act in this manner all the time. There is a tendency among politicians of all parties to present themselves as 'statesmen', above the hurly-burly of vote-catching. This can only be done when they are secure in their position or think that they are. When it happens that a politician moves on this course at the same time as a group of supporters feel that he can no longer represent them, the consequences can be devastating for the deputy involved. One Reggio member, first elected in 1958, with a number of junior ministries to his name, was not re-elected in 1976 for just this reason. Much of his support came from mafia elements in the province who had decided to switch to another candidate. At the same time, he felt that he was secure enough to aim higher than a junior ministry and therefore neglected the sort of mediation that was necessary to build up support. Instead he did not win enough preferences to be elected.

Some of the decline of the older DC leaders can be explained in these terms as well. Another striking change has taken place in the transfer of a large part of the control of public resources from national to regional government. In terms of the day to day running of the administration, the regional minister *(assessore)* has more power than the minister in Rome. Thus much of the clientelistic behaviour has been passed down to the regional offices increasing the number and quality of local focuses of power.

TWO INDIVIDUALS

1. Dario Antoniozzi

A primary index of a politician's success is his preference vote record (Table 2).

108 *Italy Today*

TABLE 2
Preferences

Date	Cs (prov)	Cz (prov)	Rc (prov)	Calabria
1953	38,168†	14,692†	8,577†	62,430*
1958	43,345†	19,019†	23,655†	72,355*
1963	46,991	20,987	12,123	80,101*
1968	57,851	23,206	27,102	108,159*
1972	55,784	20,967	23,489	100,410*
1976	43,098	15,719	17,936	76,696*
1979	40,301	14,634	12,088	67,023*

† unofficial sources
* elected

Navicella
Archivi Comunali
Local Newspapers

Before his election as a deputy Antoniozzi had held no elected post. Trained as a lawyer, he had worked in the ACLI, had been Vice-President of the Provincial Union of Co-operatives and had been a member of the board of the OVS. Spezzano, the Communist senator, was particularly scathing soon after the elections about Antoniozzi's other qualities: 'He was not number one on the list, he is not leader of the DC in Calabria, he does not have great intellectual qualities ... intellectuality and Antoniozzi are antithetical terms. He certainly does not have an exceptional character'.[32] Despite this, Antoniozzi came first in 33 *comuni* in Calabria and the *comuni* where he won large numbers of votes were those where there were branches of the *Cassa di Risparmio*. Spezzano reports being handed a leaflet with 'Vote Antoniozzi' on one side and the stamp of the bank on the other. Bank clients in Chiaravalle were invited to come into their branch supposedly to talk about loans or *cambiali* (promissory notes); the manager would then suggest that they ought to vote for Antoniozzi. In Pizzo the local administration gave 1000 lire to the needy; the money was distributed through the bank and when given out, there was the usual 'Vote Antoniozzi' slip. In other towns, loans were promised to potential voters, bank cars were used for the campaign, the telephone and bank employees were also used for the director's son.[33]

Once elected, Antoniozzi was able to maintain his position through support in the bank. Soon afterwards, the *Cassa di Risparmio della Calabria* became the *Cassa di Risparmio della Calabria e della Lucania* and an alliance was apparent between Antoniozzi and the undisputed leader of the DC in Basilicata, Emilio Colombo. This alliance has endured since the 1950s despite Antoniozzi suffering a number of rebuffs. It brought him a string of junior ministries, in particular agriculture, during the three Moro governments in the 1960s, which explains the peak of his preference votes in 1968.

The gradual falling away of his vote in 1976 and 1979 can be explained by the increased competition and Antoniozzi's own moving away from direct vote gathering politics. The competition is partly on an individual basis and partly on the interprovincial cleavage; in 1976 the DC share of the poll fell, which automatically reduced the preference votes a candidate might get; given the growth of the regional government, the other two provinces put forward strong candidates, lessening the pull of the veterans.

2. Giacomo Mancini

As with many other members of the Italian political class, Giacomo Mancini was the son of a deputy, Pietro Mancini, a lawyer and small landowner who became a socialist in the early part of the century. In 1905 Pietro Mancini founded *La Parola Socialista*, a newspaper which described the ups and downs of the Socialist Party in Cosenza until the early 1970s, and for most of that period was the party's only paper. He took part in the peasants' fights for land after the First World War and was twice elected deputy, a position he held until he was sent into internal exile in 1925. After the Second World War, Mancini was elected to the Constituent Assembly and was a rival to Nenni for the leadership of the PSI. With Nenni's consolidation of the party leadership Pietro Mancini became a life senator and went into semi-retirement until his death in 1969.

Giacomo Mancini's initial career made great use of his father's prestige, but despite the young man's shyness and difficulty at public speaking all accounts of the Forties and Fifties describe him as a hard worker and one who made great efforts to pursue certain battles, both as a party organiser and as a fighter on the electoral front. He used *La Parola Socialista* in order to attack the position of the Pisani family and other Christian Democrat dignitaries. There was a long drawn-out libel case brought against him by Alfio Pisani (eventually won by Mancini) which showed his capabilities as a campaigner.

Throughout the Fifties, Mancini was close to the Communist Party (his biographer, Orazio Barrese,[34] maintains that if it had not been for his father, he would have become a Communist after the war). With the advent of the Centre-Left, Mancini's position softened. He became a defender of the PSI's independence. As a strong local leader and above all as an important party organiser and, in a sense, Nenni's 'favourite son', Mancini was an obvious candidate for office in the Centre-Left. In the first Moro government he was Minister of Health and, more importantly, he was Minister of Public Works in Moro's second and third governments, as well as in Rumor's first and second. The first election after Mancini became a minister coincided with the unification of the PSI and PSDI. Throughout the country it was a move which was an electoral disaster; only in Calabria did the combined parties poll more than they had polled previously alone. This was entirely due to Mancini. His campaign played on the fact that for the first time the State had featured in a large and positive way in the region. The motorway, the doubling of the railway, a new line linking Cosenza with Paola, plus many other smaller public works, were actually being started rather than merely promised as before. Some were also finished. The electoral results were clear both for the party and for Mancini personally (Table 3).

TABLE 3

MANCINI PREFERENCE VOTES

Date	Cs (prov)	Cz (prov)	Rc (prov)	Calabria
1948	na	na	na	25,949*
1953	na	na	na	22,964*
1958	na	na	na	29,278*
1963	5,696	15,089	3,929	24,922*
1968	27,344	53,795	25,633	109,745*
1972	13,325	32,972	18,442	65,348*
1976	18,462	36,034	18,111	72,689*
1979	20,153	35,972	16,852	72,977*
1983	20,162	40,219	16,626	75,001*

I have not been able to find evidence of Mancini gathering votes in the same individual way that Antoniozzi and his supporters did, but many other tactics used by the Christian Democrats in the Fifites and Sixties appear in the PSI in the 1970s. It is ironic to compare the DC *Corriere delle Calabrie* in the 1950s with the PSI *Calabria Oggi* of the late Sixties and early Seventies. The one is full of accounts of the benefits that this or that *onorevole* has procured for the province, while the other is taken up with 'Mancini's speech to the Party Secretariat' or 'Mancini's speech at Crotone' (similar to the coverage given to Cassiani in the Fifties) and the projects which Socialist deputies have been sponsoring for the Region. Even more striking are the advertisements; in the former, most come from the *Cassa di Risparmio;* in the latter, they are from the Ministry of

Public Works or the Ministry of Transport (both held by Socialists over the period).

There are other methods which strike familiar chords. After the Reggio riots, Mancini became the villain of the piece for the Reggini and the right-wing daily, *La Gazzetta del Sud* (which had been a Mancini supporter), turned against him. A new paper, *Il Giornale della Calabria*, was founded and throughout its life was heavily pro-Mancini. It was sponsored by the industrialist Nino Rovelli, who at the time was setting up a chemicals factory at Lamezia largely financed with public funds. The paper itself used State funding and its print shop was opened by Mancini as Minister of Public Works. Rovelli's politics were far to the right and his business methods exciting to say the least; he used a small proportion of his own or private funding and a large proportion of money borrowed from the State. The result was a fragile and under-liquid empire which collapsed at public expense. This did not prevent an alliance between himself and Mancini to their mutual advantage.

As Minister of Public Works, Mancini was also involved in the ANAS (national road-building agency) scandal, a minor crisis by Italian standards but one which broke Mancini. He was accused of having been party to rigged auctions for public works tenders. The accusations were neither proved nor disproved and, in any case, even if there had been a payment to the Minister, the money was alleged to have gone to the party rather than Mancini personally. However the echoes of the scandal were sufficient to prevent Mancini's re-entry into government and, more importantly, his taking over the party leadership.

In his heyday, Mancini *was* the Socialist Party in Cosenza. All business went through Mancini's offices while the Provincial head-quarters was a mere ghost. His decline, as with Christian Democrat leaders, has been for infra-party reasons but, in contrast to the DC, national party movements have had more weight.

In 1980 he was not able to impose his candidate in the city elections (nor were the *Craxiani* and a compromise candidate headed the list, who was not elected). By 1983, Mancini's followers had diminished to one regional councillor (his step-daughter), one local councillor, the vice president of ESAC and the president of one USL, while the *Craxiani* included two deputies (one a minister) and a senator, six regional councillors (all ex-Manciniani), thirteen city councillors headed by the mayor plus the presidents of the IACP of Catanzaro and Reggio, the vice president of the *Cassa di Risparmio* and the president of the Chamber of Commerce. The only other faction, Signorile's, had only the ex-mayor of Cosenza and the president of the Cosenza IACP.

Nevertheless, the prestige Mancini built up over the years was demonstrated clearly in the 1983 general elections. The central party had adopted the policy of retiring its older leaders, and indeed both De Martino and Lombardi moved to the Senate. Mancini was offered a seat either in the Senate or in the European Parliament in 1984. He turned down both. Moreover, it was decided that only those who had been ministers in the previous parliament should be placed at the top of the electoral list (Mancini had not been a minister for a decade but had been number one for the previous 35 years). The resulting alphabetical list meant that Mancini was number eleven, but won the largest number of preference votes. In terms of real power, it was a Pyrrhic victory in that Craxi's faction still controlled most of the PSI in Calabria. But it showed very forcibly the strength of individual prestige over the party machine.

This tendency was confirmed when Mancini became mayor of Cosenza for a short period after the 1985 elections. Despite a high personal vote and his undoubted prestige among members of all parties but his own, he was not able to build and maintain a consensus within the city government.

Given the changes that the PSI has gone through in Calabria, it is not for nothing that an old Socialist militant complained that the party had become 'a little DC'.[35]

CONCLUSIONS

The picture of Calabrian, and to a large extent, southern politics which I have described is one in which political power is channelled through individuals and groups rather than through clearly defined ideologies or pressure groups. This is not to say that the parties are irrelevant; on the contrary they are the key to any form of success. Nor can we maintain that ideology is irrelevant to winning the vote. Organised Catholicism played an important part in producing DC support in the Forties and Fifties as did its complement, anti-Communism. The MSI success after the Reggio riots had little to do with electors' hopes for immediate material gain, nor did the Communist increase of the mid-Seventies. Within the parties, personal prestige rather than the possibility of granting favours also acted as a magnet for preference votes (Mancini was the main example), as did local 'patriotism'.

There are, moreover, frequent examples of politicians acting for the benefit of groups wider than their direct *clientela*. The road-building programme implemented by Mancini for the whole of Calabria is one example, and Antoniozzi's efforts to upgrade the Cosenza theatre and library to national status (which meant a great increase in State funding for both institutions) and the foundation of a school for restoration in

Cozenza (which gave more wealth and prestige to the whole city) are others. In the same way, the work of the two mayor-deputies, Principe (PSI) and Belluscio (PSDI), at the national level reflects on the whole of their respective villages.

All this means is that not all party and preference votes are clientelistic. The personal element is still very strong. It is indicative that two of the apparently party newspapers which have been quoted do not in fact belong to the parties. *La Parola Socialista* was founded by Pietro Mancini and the masthead then belonged to Giacomo; the PSI wanted to buy it but Mancini would not sell. *Democrazia Cristiana*, despite its name was founded by Don Luigi Nicoletti and was his personal property. After his severe criticism of the local *Fanfaniani* in 1956, another, 'official', paper was founded.

While the personal element in Calabrian politics is not diminishing, there does seem to be a decrease in the stability of the individuals involved and the purely prestige element is becoming less influential. This is a tendency noted by other observers of the South; the competition for political success becomes harder as the potential *clientela* become more selective. A favour lasts for only one election; if the goods are not delivered, then the voter goes elsewhere. The bank is no longer the property of one faction and a *clientela* built up through office in the regional government has to be cultivated at the national level, otherwise it will be lost. An example of this last point was the Reggino deputy, Vico Ligato, who had gone through a fairly rapid rise and fall. He started as the protegé of the Reggio deputy Vincelli, a *Fanfaniano*, was elected to the Region in 1970, and by using the regional government was able to build up more influence than his master. In the 1976 elections he was able to put up his own candidate who was elected while Vincelli was not. By 1979 he felt powerful enough to move to Rome, stood, and came in second only just behind the ex-minister Misasi and way ahead of Antoniozzi and other ex-deputies. Since then as a backbench deputy (the DC has the practice of not giving junior ministries to deputies in their first parliament), he has had considerably less power than he had as a Regional minister. On the 1983 elections, his preference votes sank; he gave up his post in Parliament to become the chairman of the new State Railways Board.

The example of Ligato does however show the importance of the regional government in developing a power base. Another Christian Democrat, Carmelo Pujia, whose career is an epitome of modern clientelism, was criticised and despised by members of all parties, including his own. A Communist paper described him as 'a man of power, unscrupulous, with a crude cultural background';[36] a Christian

Democrat interviewee called him 'the ten per cent President [of the Province]'.[37] In the Fifties he worked for a Consortium in Lamezia headed by the DC deputy Foderaro, but was not given a steady job. He complained to another Christian Democrat, Ernesto Pucci, then a member of the board of the Opera Sila, who found him a job that same day. When Pucci became a deputy, Pujia joined his secretariat. He became a provincial councillor in 1964 with responsibility for Public Works, as well as taking the post of Deputy Secretary of the DC. His position in the Opera Sila was used to place supporters, a tactic he used when the then president of the province moved on to the Region. By 1972 he was strong enough to field his own candidate in the general elections, Guido Mantella, who has ben re-elected ever since. In 1975, he stood for the region and collected different posts despite a theoretical incompatibility.[38] From then on until his own election in 1983, he gave his support to various different factions in Rome according to which is able to deliver the most. In the scandal over bribes for building permits in Catanzaro, Pujia was not directly involved, although one of his supporters (who was supposed to stand for parliament) was. This meant that Pujia stood himself. He won the second highest number of preference votes (after the national leader, Riccardo Misasi).

With this type of politician in the DC (and in the 1980s in large parts of the PSI as well), the ideological and policy elements are reduced to a minimum. It does not mean, however, that their behaviour is the accepted norm for politics in Calabria. I have already mentioned how Pujia was criticised by party colleagues. There are examples of how Christian Democrats, as well as the opposition, set standards in their public utterances which are in stark contrast to the way the game is actually played.

There have been moments in the last forty years when attempts have been made to reduce not only corruption but also clientelistic vote-gathering. To the question in an interview 'What other problems must be faced immediately?', the new mayor in Reggio in 1977 gave the following answers:

> The personnel and the waste . . . no more personal cars and drivers . . . Then there are the 250 streetcleaners (out of a total of 550) who must be found since no one knows where they have got to, and also a hundred or so traffic wardens . . .
>
> [Interviewer] Be careful, Mr Mayor, that way there is the risk of losing votes.
>
> [Mayor] It's a calculated risk. Sooner or later the method has to change.[39]

A decade after that interview the city administration of Reggio was under suspicion for suspected mafia involvement and the Regional Savings bank in Cosenza was being run by a Bank of Italy appointee in order to repair the damage done by loans granted on a political basis rather than a banking basis. Indeed the method has changed since 1977 but not in the direction hoped for by the mayor of Reggio.

NOTES

1   Some authors make strong correlations between electoral system and the degree of spoils sharing; for a recent example, see Lancaster Thomas D. 'Electoral Structures and Pork Barrel Politics' *International Political Science Review* Vol. 7 (1) 1986, pp. 67–81.

2   Often the process is the reverse of the way I have suggested: 'I vote Bianchi because he helps me; if he changes lobby, faction, even party, then I will follow.' This personal attachment is one of the essential elements of clientelism.

3   Cf. Senate, *Discussioni*, 2 December 1953, p. 2452.

4   Op. Cit., pp. 2454–5.

5   *Parola Socialista*, LIII (1), 5 January 1958, p. 3.

6   *Risveglio Cosentino*,(14), 25 October 1957, p. 1.

7   *Risveglio Cosentino*, (15), 31 October 1961, p. 2.

8   *questaCalabria*, (5), 24 April 1976, pp. 8–9.

9   *Repubblica*, 17 December 1986, p. 6.

10   *Repubblica*, 14 march 1987, p. 38, 15 March 1987, p. 4, 17 March 1987, p. 48.

11   M. Caciagli (ed.), *Democrazia cristiana e potere nel Mezzogiorno. Il sistema democristiana a Catania*, Florence, Guaraldi, 1977.

12   *Battaglia Calabra*, IX (32), 1 August 1955.

13   *Parola Socialista*, 10 November 1957.

14   Interview, member of Cosenza IACP, May 1983.

15   *Repubblica*, 4 February 1987, p. 7.

16   *Messaggero*, 17 January 1987, p. 18.

17   *Repubblica*, 12 March 1987, p. 13.

18   *Calabria Oggi*, 17 July 1970.

19   Arca' Francesco *Mafia, potere, malgoverno*, Roma, Newton Compton, 1979, p. 116 and Mannino Saverio *La strage di Razza*, Roma, Edizioni Dimensione 80, pp. 113–24.

20   Walston James 'Electoral Politics in Southern Calabria' in *Contemporary Crises*, 5 1981, pp. 417–95.

21   Tribunale di Reggio Calabria, Ufficio dell'Istruzione Penale, Ordinanza nel Procedimento Penale n. 60/78 contro De Stefano, +59, p. 33.

22   *Calabria* (Regional Assembly Monthly), XV, No. 22, February 1987, pp. 32–41.

23   Author's interview, February 1982.

24   Arlacchi Pino 'Gangsterismo e società a Cosenza: un'ipotesi interpretativa' in AA.VV. *Gangsters a Cosenza*, Cosenza, Effesette, 1982, p. 36.

25   *questaCalabria*, (12), 1 August 1976, p. 3.

26   *questaCalabria*, 4 July 1976, p. 14; confirmed by Reale in an interview with the author in December 1983.

27   Borzomati Pietro *La Calabria in età contemporanea*, Reggio Calabria, Editori Meridionali Riuniti, 1977, pp. 116–7.

28   Mauro Calise and Renato Mannheimer, 'Misurare i governi: la distribuzione territoriale
     dei governanti italiani 1948–78', in *Il Mulino*, July–August 1981.
29   *questaCalabria*, (2), 13 March 1976, p. 9.
30   Author's interview, May 1983.
31   Author's interview, May 1983.
32   Senate, *Discussioni*, op cit., pp. 2455–6.
33   Ibid., p. 2461.
34   Orazio Barrese, *Mancini*, Milano, Feltrinelli, 1976.
35   Author's interview, April 1983.
36   *questaCalabria*, (3), 13 March 1976, p. 5.
37   Author's interview, May 1983.
38   *questaCalabria*, (3), 27 March 1976, p. 11.
39   *questaCalabria*, (31), 13 June 1977, p. 6.

NOTES ON CONTRIBUTORS

JOHN EISENHAMMER read PPE at Christ Church, Oxford. After completing a doctoral thesis on contemporary French politics at Nuffield College, Oxford, he went in 1983 to the *Fondazione Basso*, Rome, where he wrote on various aspects of Italian politics and carried out research for the Western European Steel Project, based at the European University Institute, Florence. He now works as a current affairs producer for the BBC World Service.

PAUL FURLONG has degrees from Rome, Oxford and Reading and is Lecturer in Politics at the University of Hull. He has published widely in the field of contemporary Italian politics, and in particular on the Christian Democrat Party, on religion in Italian politics, and on Italian public policy. He is currently working on State finance and industrial policy in Italy.

JOHN POLLARD is Senior Lecturer in Italian History at Cambridge College of Arts and Technology and a member of the executive committee of the Association for the Study of Modern Italy (ASMI). Among his publications is *The Vatican and Italian Fascism: A Study in Conflict*, Cambridge University Press, 1985.

GEOFFREY PRIDHAM is Reader in European Politics at the University of Bristol. He is the author of several books on politics in Italy and Europe, amongst which are: *Christian Democracy in Western Germany: The CDU/CSU in Government and Opposition, 1945-76* (1977), *The Nature of the Italian Party System: A Regional Case-study* (1981), *Transnational Party Cooperation and European Integration: The Process Towards Direct Elections* (1981). He is the editor of *The New Mediterranean Democracies: Regime Transition in Spain, Greece and Portugal* (1984). He is currently writing a book on *Political Parties and Coalitional Behaviour in Italy: An Interpretative Study*, and editing *Political Parties and Coalitional Behaviour in Western Europe*.

LUISA QUARTERMAINE is Lecturer in Italian at the University of Exeter. A graduate of Bocconi University, Milan, she has published on Renaissance literature and iconography, on contemporary Italian literature, Italian cinema and culture under Fascism. Editor of the Italian Civilisation section of the *Exeter Tapes* series, she is currently researching on the activities of the Ministry of Culture during the Republic of Salò 1943–5. She is a member of the executive committee of the Association for the Study of Modern Italy (ASMI) and of the Associazione Internazionale dei Professori di Italiano (AIPI); she is also Vice-Chairman of the Association of Teachers of Italian (ATI).

MARTIN SLATER is Lecturer in the Department of Government at the

University of Essex. Since 1983 he has also been Visiting Professor in the Faculty of Political Science at the University of Turin. He has written widely on migration in Western Europe, the EEC, and Italian politics. He is currently engaged in research in party ideology and coalition behaviour in post-war Italy.

JAMES WALSTON is Lecturer in Political Science at the University of Maryland, University College (European Division) with a BA and PhD from Cambridge and a *Diploma di Perfezionamento* from Rome. He has published on civil rights, Italian politics, mafia and camorra in British, Italian and American journals. He is the author of *Roads to Rome. Mafia and Clientelism in Post-war Calabria*. He has written for the *Guardian*, the *New Statesman* and the *Observer* as well as acting as a consultant on Italian politics for Granada and HTV.

INDEX

119

120